The Battle of Britain

Books in the Battles Series:

The Battle of Belleau Wood

The Battle of Britain

The Battle of Gettysburg

The Battle of Hastings

The Battle of Marathon

The Battle of Midway

The Battle of Waterloo

The Battle of Zama

The Inchon Invasion

The Invasion of Normandy

★ ★ ★ Battles of World War II ★ ★ ★

The Battle of Britain

by Earle Rice Jr.

Lucent Books, P.O. Box 289011, San Diego, CA 92198-9011

Library of Congress Cataloging-in-Publication Data

Rice, Earle.
  The battle of Britain / by Earle Rice, Jr.
    p. cm. — (Battles of World War II)
  Includes bibliographical references and index.
  ISBN 1-56006-414-5 (lib. bdg. : alk. paper)
  1. Britain, Battle of, 1940—Juvenile literature. I. Title. II. Series
  D756.5.B7R53 1996
  940.54'211—dc20   95-16624
                                                              CIP

Contents

Foreword   6

Chronology of Events   8

Introduction: England Stands Alone   9

Chapter 1: First Phase: The Battle Begins   16

Chapter 2: August Overture: Luftwaffe Warm-Up   31

Chapter 3: August 13–15: Three Days of the Eagle   41

Chapter 4: Second Phase: The Focus Shifts   55

Chapter 5: September 15: Battle of Britain Day   65

Chapter 6: Third Phase: Winding Down and Summing Up   76

Glossary   85

For Further Reading   87

Works Consulted   88

Appendix: Principal Aircraft in the Battle of Britain   89

Index   92

Picture Credits   95

About the Author   96

Foreword

Almost everyone would agree with William Tecumseh Sherman that war "is all hell." Yet the history of war, and battles in particular, is so fraught with the full spectrum of human emotion and action that it becomes a microcosm of the human experience. Soldiers' lives are condensed and crystallized in a single battle. As Francis Miller explains in his *Photographic History of the Civil War* when describing the war wounded, "It is sudden, the transition from marching bravely at morning on two sound legs, grasping your rifle in two sturdy arms, to lying at nightfall under a tree with a member forever gone."

Decisions made on the battlefield can mean the lives of thousands. A general's pique or indigestion can result in the difference between life and death. Some historians speculate, for example, that Napoleon's fateful defeat at Waterloo was due to the beginnings of stomach cancer. His stomach pain may have been the reason that the normally decisive general was sluggish and reluctant to move his troops. And what kept George McClellan from winning battles during the Civil War? Some scholars and contemporaries believe that it was simple cowardice and fear. Others argue that he felt a gut-wrenching unwillingness to engage in the war of attrition that was characteristic of that particular conflict.

Battle decisions can be magnificently brilliant and horribly costly. At the Battle of Thaspus in 47 B.C., for example, Julius Caesar, facing a numerically superior army, shrewdly ordered his troops onto a narrow strip of land bordering the sea. Just as he expected, his enemy thought he had accidentally trapped himself and divided their forces to surround his troops. By dividing their army, his enemy had given Caesar the strategic edge he needed to defeat them. Other battle orders result in disaster, as in the case of the Battle at Balaklava during the Crimean War in 1854. A British general gave the order to attack a force of withdrawing enemy Russians. But confusion in relaying the order resulted in the 670 men of the Light Brigade's charging in the wrong direction into certain death by heavy enemy cannon fire. Battles are the stuff of history on the grandest scale—their outcomes often determine whether nations are enslaved or liberated.

Moments in battles illustrate the best and worst of human character. In the feeling of terror and the us-versus-them attitude that accompanies war, the enemy can be dehumanized and treated with a contempt that is considered repellent in times of peace. At Wounded Knee, the distrust and anticipation of violence that grew between the Native Americans and American soldiers led to the senseless killing of ninety men, women, and children. And who can forget My Lai, where the deaths of old men, women, and children at the hands of American soldiers shocked an America already disillusioned with the Vietnam War. The murder of six million Jews will remain burned into the human conscience forever as the measure of man's inhumanity to man. These horrors cannot be forgotten. And yet, under the terrible conditions of battle, one can find acts of bravery, kindness, and altruism. During the Battle of Midway, the members of Torpedo Squadron 8, flying in hopelessly antiquated planes and without the benefit of air protection from fighters, tried bravely to fulfill their mission—to destroy the *Kido Butai,* the Japanese Carrier Striking Force. Without air support, the squadron was immediately set upon by Japanese fighters. Nevertheless, each bomber tried valiantly to hit his target. Each failed. Every man but one died in the effort. But by keeping the Japanese fighters busy, the squadron bought time and delayed further Japanese fighter attacks. In the aftermath of the Battle of Isandhlwana in South Africa in 1879, a force of thousands of Zulu warriors trapped a contingent of British troops in a small trading post. After repeated bloody attacks in which many died on both sides, the Zulus, their final victory certain, granted the remaining British their lives as a gesture of respect for their bravery. During World War I, American troops were so touched by the fate of French war orphans that they took up a collection to help them. During the Civil War, soldiers of the North and South would briefly forget that they were enemies and share smokes and coffee across battle lines during the endless nights. These acts seem all the more dramatic, more uplifting, because they indicate that people can continue to behave with humanity when faced with inhumanity.

Lucent Books' Battles Series highlights the vast range of the human character revealed in the ordeal of war. Dramatic narrative describes in exciting and accurate detail the commanders, soldiers, weapons, strategies, and maneuvers involved in each battle. Each volume includes a comprehensive historical context, explaining what brought the parties to war, the events leading to the battle, what factors made the battle important, and the effects it had on the larger war and later events.

The Battles Series also includes a chronology of important dates that gives students an overview, at a glance, of each battle. Sidebars create a broader context by adding enlightening details on leaders, institutions, customs, warships, weapons, and armor mentioned in the narration. Every volume contains numerous maps that allow readers to better visualize troop movements and strategies. In addition, numerous primary and secondary source quotations drawn from both past historical witnesses and modern historians are included. These quotations demonstrate to readers how and where historians derive information about past events. Finally, the volumes in the Battles Series provide a launching point for further reading and research. Each book contains a bibliography designed for student research, as well as a second bibliography that includes the works the author consulted while compiling the book.

Above all, the Battles Series helps illustrate the words of Herodotus, the fifth-century B.C. Greek historian now known as the "father of history." In the opening lines of his great chronicle of the Greek and Persian Wars, the world's first battle book, he set for himself this goal: "To preserve the memory of the past by putting on record the astonishing achievements both of our own and of other peoples; and more particularly, to show how they came into conflict."

Chronology of Events

June 28, 1919
Treaty of Versailles is signed.

January 30, 1933
Hitler is appointed chancellor of Germany, marking the birth of the Third Reich, or European empire headed by Germany.

January 30, 1937
Hitler addresses the Reichstag and proclaims "the withdrawal of the German signature" from the Versailles treaty.

March 12, 1938
Germany annexes Austria.

October 1, 1938
Germany occupies Sudetenland sector of Czechoslovakia.

September 1, 1939
Germany invades Poland.

September 3, 1939
England and France declare war on Germany.

October 3, 1939
BEF (British Expeditionary Force) takes up positions along Franco-Belgian frontier.

April 9, 1940
Germany invades Norway and Denmark.

May 10, 1940
Germany launches huge offensive on the Western Front.

May 14, 1940
Holland surrenders to German invaders.

May 26–June 4, 1940
BEF and French forces evacuate at Dunkirk.

May 28, 1940
Belgium surrenders to Germany.

June 4–8, 1940
Allies withdraw from Norway.

June 14, 1940
Nazi storm troopers march into Paris.

June 24, 1940
France falls.

July 3, 1940
Preparations begin for Operation Sea Lion, the invasion of England.

July 10, 1940
Battle of Britain begins.

July 16, 1940
Hitler issues War Directive No. 16, which gives official birth to Operation Sea Lion.

August 1, 1940
Hitler issues War Directive No. 17, ordering the immediate destruction of the RAF (Royal Air Force) by the German air force (Luftwaffe).

August 11, 1940
"Sailor Malan's August Eleventh."

August 13, 1940
Adler Tag (Eagle Day).

August 15, 1940
Massive Luftwaffe raid on Britain by Air Fleets 2, 3, and 5.

August 18, 1940
First phase of Battle of Britain ends.

August 23–24, 1940
London is bombed.

August 24, 1940
Second phase of Battle of Britain begins; RAF bombs Berlin.

September 7, 1940
The London "blitz" begins and continues for fifty-seven nights.

September 15, 1940
Battle of Britain Day.

September 17, 1940
Hitler postpones Operation Sea Lion.

September 27, 1940
Second phase of Battle of Britain ends on the RAF's "third greatest day."

September 28, 1940
Third phase of Battle of Britain begins.

September 30, 1940
Luftwaffe makes last big daylight attack on London.

October 31, 1940
Battle of Britain ends.

INTRODUCTION

England Stands Alone

"When Marshal Foch heard of the signing of the Peace Treaty of Versailles at the close of World War I, he observed with singular accuracy: 'This is not Peace. It is an Armistice for twenty years.'" So wrote Winston Churchill in *The Gathering Storm*, the first book in his six-volume account of World War II.

As Churchill points out, Marshal Ferdinand Foch, France's finest soldier of the twentieth century, couldn't have been more correct. The peace terms established at Versailles on June 28, 1919, laid the groundwork for a series of events that led directly to the outbreak of World War II. The peace terms of the First World War, which had been called the "war to end all wars" succeeded only in keeping a potentially explosive situation on hold.

The Treaty of Versailles

When World War I began in 1914, the opposing forces were the Central Powers (Germany, Austria-Hungary, and Turkey) and the Allies (England, France, Russia, Belgium, Serbia, Serbia's neighbor Montenegro, and Japan). During the course of the war, additional nations joined, or were conquered by, one side or the other. After the Armistice of November 11, 1918, brought an end to the fighting, all the victorious nations except Russia gathered in Paris to discuss the terms of the peace agreement that would later be signed at Versailles.

In any peace settlement, the winners of a war try to prevent the losers from ever starting another one. All the Central Powers except

Germany had surrendered by July 1918, so at Versailles in 1919 the Allies focused on Germany and tried to remove that nation's capability for making war. Germany, in exchange for peace, was forced to accept an agreement that it could not possibly honor.

In part, the treaty stripped Germany of its colonies and some of its land in Europe. It insisted that Germany confess its sole responsibility for the war. And it established size limitations for Germany's armed forces. The treaty further demanded that Germany pay the Allied nations about $100 billion (over $600 billion today) for war damages. The demand for such harsh reparations had a crippling effect on the German economy.

Already weak from four years of war, Germany's postwar economy stood little chance of making good on the claims set against it. Such demands could only cause the war-weary Germans more hardships and suffering. The Germans also deeply resented having to accept total blame. They had neither caused nor fought the war alone.

A network of alliances designed to keep peace in Europe had turned the continent into two armed camps. Germany presided over one camp, France over the other. This state of war readiness led inevitably to the clash of aligned nations. The assassination of the heir to the Austro-Hungarian throne, Archduke Franz Ferdinand, and his wife, in Bosnian Sarajevo provided the spark that lit the fuse of European discontent. An explosive chain reaction followed. Because the assassin was a Serbian national, Austria-Hungary threatened to invade Serbia. Russia, allied to the Serbs, mobilized to counter the Austro-Hungarian threat. Germany then mobilized to aid Austria-Hungary. France mobilized in turn to aid Russia. Britain rushed to join France. And so on. Ultimately, instead of preserving the peace, the alliances involved most of Europe in a bloody war.

There can be little doubt that Germany deserved a share of the blame but certainly not total responsibility for the conflict. Had calmer heads prevailed on both sides, the war might have been averted. History has since accorded a share of guilt to the other nations that rushed to war, as well. In 1919, however, the victorious Allies determined to place the blame on Germany, which had been the principal military and economic power in Europe.

Fearful that Germany might regain sufficient strength to wage another war, the vindictive and unforgiving victors exacted harsh measures against a defeated enemy in the cause of a lasting peace. Thus did the Allies all but guarantee World War II.

The Third Reich

During the 1920s, Germany struggled with an unstable government under a constitution drawn up in accordance with the terms of the Treaty of Versailles. As political parties on both the left and the right of this new government, called the Weimar Republic, competed for control, inflation soared and middle-class savings were destroyed. Inevitably, economic depression set in. The once-proud German people, first defeated and now deprived, looked at what their lives had become and saw only doom and despair. When a former corporal in the German army promised to restore Germany to its glory, Germans listened.

And a new German empire, the Third Reich, was born.

On January 30, 1933, the aging president of the Weimar Republic, Paul von Hindenburg, appointed Adolf Hitler as his chancellor, or principal administrator. As chancellor, Hitler, the head of the National Socialist German Workers' (Nazi) Party, assumed the full powers of a dictator. Boasting that his reich would last for a thousand years, the former corporal, who formerly had gone by the name of Adolf Schicklgruber, immediately started leading Germany down paths of dubious glory.

Ignoring the terms of Versailles, Hitler secretly rebuilt Germany's armed forces into the most powerful military machine ever assembled on this planet. From a position of strength, he then declared Germany's need for more living space, or *Lebensraum*. Specifically, Hitler wanted to reclaim all the lands lost at Versailles and to acquire any additional lands he considered necessary for Germany's well-being.

Lebensraum

In his book *Mein Kampf* (*My Struggle*), Hitler wrote: "Only an adequate large space on this earth assures a nation of freedom of existence." He felt convinced that "traditions" and prejudices should not be considered. Rather, he said that the Nazis "must find the courage to gather our people and their strength for an advance along the road that will lead this people from its present restricted living space to new land and soil." Concluding his thoughts on *Lebensraum,* Hitler cautioned that the Nazis must hold without fail to their aim "to secure for the German people the land and soil to which they are entitled."

Hitler, in a speech to the legislature, the Reichstag, on January 30, 1937, gave formal notice that Germany would no longer observe the terms of the Versailles treaty. He stated that a great power could not accept such restrictions. This announcement prepared the way for Germany to start expanding its borders in the name of *Lebensraum*.

On March 12, 1938, Germany first moved to annex Austria, then occupied the Sudetenland sector of Czechoslovakia in October. The rest of Europe chose not to interfere with Hitler's expansion. He next extended his occupation of the Sudetenland to include all of Czechoslovakia. Other European countries continued a hands-off policy, hoping to curb Hitler's aggression

When Adolf Hitler first began to invade the countries bordering Germany, few leaders in Europe wished to involve their nations in another war. This reluctance fed Hitler's dreams of taking over the world.

The "Thousand-Year Reich"

William L. Shirer, the brilliant author, journalist, and chronicler of Nazi Germany, wrote: "The Third Reich which was born on January 30, 1933, Hitler boasted, would endure for a thousand years, and in Nazi parlance it was often referred to as the 'Thousand-Year Reich.' It lasted twelve years and four months, but in that flicker of time, as history goes, it caused an eruption on this earth more violent and shattering than any previously experienced, raising the German people to heights of power they had not known in more than a millennium, making them at one time the masters of Europe from the Atlantic to the Volga, from the North Cape to the Mediterranean, and then plunging them to the depths of destruction and desolation at the end of a world war which their nation had cold-bloodedly provoked and during which it instituted a reign of terror over the conquered people which, in its calculated butchery of human life and the human spirit, outdid all the savage oppressions of the previous ages.

"The man who founded the Third Reich, who ruled it ruthlessly and often with uncommon shrewdness, who led it to such dizzy heights and to such a sorry end, was a person of undoubted, if evil, genius."

German troops march into Austria to annex that nation in March 1938. Hitler's moves into Austria did not upset the rest of Europe because many people, including the Austrians themselves, saw it as logical.

through peaceful negotiations or outright appeasement. But Hitler's pursuit of more "living space" was not to be deterred by talk. On September 1, 1939, Hitler's armies struck suddenly across Germany's eastern border and invaded Poland.

Two days later, England and France declared war on Germany. The United States immediately declared itself neutral and would remain so for another twenty-seven months. In Europe, however, the most destructive war in the history of humankind had begun.

Blitzkrieg

Hitler's *blitzkrieg*, or lightning war, forced Poland to surrender on September 28. On October 3, I Corps of the British Expeditionary Force (BEF) moved across the English Channel and took up positions along the Franco-Belgian frontier. In the early days, the action was far from frenzied: speakers of English used the term "phony war." To the French it was *la drôle de guerre* (funny little war), and to the Germans, *der Sitzkrieg* (sitting war). For several months it seemed as if neither side wanted to anger the other by mounting an offensive. The limited action served as a blessing for the Royal Air Force (RAF), whose aircraft matched up poorly against the German *Luftwaffe* (air force) machines both in quality and in numbers.

Although the British Hurricane and Spitfire fighters held their own with the Messerschmitt Me 109 fighters, at the start the Ger-

mans had far more of the Me 109s. The numbers gap forced the RAF to throw many outdated Boulton-Paul Defiant two-seat fighters into the early battles. The Germans destroyed the Defiants in great numbers. Over time, however, the RAF would close the gap in Hurricane and Spitfire production.

The war broadened with Germany's invasion of Norway and Denmark on April 9, 1940. Denmark surrendered at once without a fight. Then, on May 10, Germany launched a huge offensive on the Western Front, an arc that followed Germany's western border from Belgium at the North Sea to Switzerland. The offensive comprised two major drives, supported by seventy-five divisions and hundreds of aircraft. One German thrust attacked the Lowlands of Holland and Belgium; the other skirted the vaunted French Maginot Line, a heavily fortified, two-hundred-mile stretch of land that ran along the Franco-German border from the Swiss border to Montmédy, France.

Construction of the Maginot Line had begun in 1923. This system of steel and concrete gun emplacements was designed to withstand any future German aggressions. In May 1940, the Germans made no effort to crash the line, however; they simply went around it. Why French strategists had not foreseen such a

(Right) German troops successfully attack the Maginot Line in 1940. (Top) "The thin blue line"—the pilots (and Hurricanes) of the RAF that would attempt to keep Hitler from invading England and completing his takeover of Western Europe.

"Force England to Her Knees"

On May 23, 1939, Adolf Hitler met with his military chiefs in Berlin. He told them that Germany's economic problems could be solved only by acquiring more *Lebensraum*—living space. He acknowledged, however, that this was impossible "without invading other countries or attacking other people's possessions."

Hitler realized that further German aggression in Europe would ultimately involve a confrontation with England and France. War was inevitable, therefore Germany must prepare. Hitler said:

The aim must be to deal the enemy a smashing or a finally decisive blow right from the start. Considerations of right or wrong, or of treaties, do not enter into the matter.

Preparations must be made for a *long war as well as* for a surprise *attack*, and every possible intervention by England on the Continent must be smashed.

The Army must occupy the positions important for the fleet and the Luftwaffe. If we succeed in occupying and securing Holland and Belgium, as well as defeating France, the basis for a successful war against England has been created.

The Luftwaffe can then closely blockade England from western France and the fleet can undertake the wider blockade with submarines.

"The aim," Hitler emphasized, "will always be to force England to her knees."

---

maneuver remains a mystery, especially since the Germans had nearly captured Paris in a similar move during World War I.

In England, Neville Chamberlain—old, tired, and disappointed at his failure to negotiate a peace settlement with the Germans—resigned as Britain's prime minister and was replaced by Winston Churchill. Meanwhile, German panzer (armored) units smashed through Allied defenses in the Ardennes region of Belgium and France, while droves of panzers swept across the Lowlands. Holland surrendered on May 14, with Belgium following on May 28.

Dunkirk

The advancing Germans then forced the evacuation of 338,226 British and French troops at the French port of Dunkirk, beginning on May 26 and ending on June 4. The Allied armies left behind most of their weapons and equipment, including huge stacks of rifles. Despite the terrible military setback, Winston Churchill spoke for all Britons in an address to the House of Commons. With the prospect of a German invasion of England rapidly becoming a reality, Churchill said, "We shall never surrender."

Thousands of French and British troops are evacuated off Dunkirk's beaches in June 1940.

At the same time, the Allies, having fought a losing battle in Norway, finally withdrew their troops during June 4–8. The next day, Norway's king ordered all Norwegian forces to surrender.

The seemingly unstoppable German war machine stormed into Paris on June 14. Tears streamed down the faces of thousands of French people lining the Champs Élysées, as Nazi storm troopers goose-stepped into the city. France surrendered on June 24. And Hitler immediately declared, "The war in the west is won."

England Stands Alone

England now stood alone in Europe against the blitzing Germans. Across the narrow English Channel, Hitler looked ahead with full confidence to Operation Sea Lion, his code name for the invasion of England. Threatened with extinction, Britons, with jutting chins, began preparing to face what Winston Churchill so aptly called "their finest hour."

☆ ☆ ☆ ☆ ☆

"We Shall Never Surrender"

On the evening of June 4, 1940, following the successful evacuation at Dunkirk, Winston Churchill, in an address to the House of Commons, warned: "We must be careful not to assign to this deliverance the attributes of a victory. Wars are not won by evacuations. But there was a victory inside this deliverance, which should be noted," Churchill wrote later. "It was gained by the Air Force. . . . They [the Germans] tried hard, and they were beaten back; they were frustrated in their task. We got the [British] Army away; and they have paid fourfold for any losses which they have inflicted. . . ." Britain's prime minister went on to deliver one of history's most dramatic and inspiring speeches. "We shall go on to the end, we shall fight in France, we shall fight in the seas and oceans, we shall fight with growing confidence and growing strength in the air, we shall defend our island, whatever the cost shall be, we shall fight on the landing-grounds, we shall fight in the fields and in the streets, we shall fight in the hills; we shall never surrender, and even if, which I do not for a moment believe, this island or a large part of it, were subjugated and starving, then our Empire beyond the seas, armed and guarded by the British Fleet, would carry on the struggle, until, in God's good time, the New World, with all its power and might, steps forth to the rescue and the liberation of the Old."

CHAPTER ONE

First Phase: The Battle Begins

Somewhere over Weymouth, England, July 9, 1940, Pilot Officer David M. Crook and two companions of the Royal Air Force's 609 Squadron caught sight of the enemy for the first time: twin-engined Messerschmitt Me 110 fighters, about nine of them. The Me 110s were diving down from behind and coming on fast. Prickling with excitement, Crook blurted out a warning over his radio telephone, but his two companions never heard the message. New, inexperienced pilots, they had forgotten to switch their radio telephone sets from "transmit" to "receive." In the dizzying confusion that followed, one of the other pilots—Crook's roommate—was shot down. The third man escaped, but just barely.

Crook himself managed to spin around fast and draw close to one of the 110s. He thumbed his firing button. His Spitfire's guns—eight .303-inch Browning machine guns, each capable of cranking off 1,350 rounds a minute—chattered in response. Crook later described their deadly power with childlike wonder:

> I gave him a terrific blast of fire at very close range. Even in the heat of the moment I well remember my amazement at the shattering effect of my fire. Pieces flew off his fuselage and cockpit covering. A stream of smoke appeared from the engine. A moment later a great sheet of flame licked out from the engine cowling and he dived vertically. The flames enveloped the whole machine. He went straight down, for about 5,000 feet, till he was just a shapeless burning mass of wreckage.

Fascinated by the sight of his first victim, Crook followed him down and saw him hit the sea with a great burst of white foam.

"I had often wondered what would be my feelings when killing somebody like this, and especially when seeing them go down in flames," he later commented. "I was rather surprised to reflect afterwards that my own feeling had been one of considerable elation—and a sort of bewildered surprise because it had all been so easy."

Returning to his base at Salisbury, Crook bumped down in "a perfectly bloody" landing. He recalled his body shaking and his voice trembling "due, I suppose, to a fairly even mixture of fright, intense excitement, and a sort of reckless exhilaration." Such feelings would become routine over the long summer, and the young pilot would learn to deal with them. Handling the loss of companions and friends, however, would take a lot of learning.

Crook recalled going back to the room that he had shared with the pilot shot down that morning. "Everything was just the same as Peter and I had left it. . . . His towel was still in the window where he had thrown it during our hurried dressing."

Everything in the room had remained the same. Everything else had changed. The next day, July 10, 1940, would be the date marked by future historians as the start of the Battle of Britain. The battle was already over for Peter. For Pilot Officer David M. Crook, it was just beginning.

Britain Braces

After the fall of France, Hitler, with his troops assembling along the English Channel coast, found himself wondering about his next move. The Nazi military machine had swept across Europe so fast it surprised even him. He never doubted the might of his *Wehrmacht* (army) or the Luftwaffe, but he had expected much stronger resistance, especially from France. Hitler's generals, for their part, had been too busy directing troops in battle to devote time to long-range planning. As a result, the German blitzkrieg had outrun German strategy. Now, Hitler faced the unusual problem of deciding what to do next with his undefeated—and presently idle—army.

If Hitler had doubts about his next move, Winston Churchill had none. In an emotional address to a crowded House of Commons on June 18, he spoke of Britain's "inflexible resolve to continue the war." He warned that the battle of France was over and that the Battle of Britain was about to begin. The fate of a nation hung on his words.

"The whole fury and might of the enemy must very soon be turned on us," he said in a soft, halting voice. "Hitler knows that he will have to break us in this island or lose the war." As he neared the end of his message, his voice grew louder, stronger. "Let us therefore brace ourselves to our duty, and so bear ourselves that, if the British Empire and its Commonwealth last for a thousand years, men will say, 'This was their finest hour.'"

After the fall of France to the Nazis, Winston Churchill knew that Hitler would attempt a takeover of England next.

The Battle of Britain

Sir Hugh Dowding wrote:

The Battle of Britain was purely defensive.

It was not fought to win a victory, but to avoid immediate and irretrievable defeat. When it was all over, very few people realized that a victory had been won at all, because another battle, the *night* attacks on our towns and factories, was still raging.

What Hitler required was command of the air *by day* to enable his fleet of small craft to attempt the crossing from the Channel ports, so that he might have air cover during the daylight. This he never attained, and so the attempt had to be abandoned.

The night attacks could not be checked until new equipment in the shape of radar and aircraft was provided. A deficiency of aircraft was avoided owing to the genius of Lord Beaverbrook, and a deficiency of pilots through the cooperation of various allied and friendly nations. It was a hard fought battle, fought with bravery and determination by both sides.

In recognition of the roles played by Dowding and Park in the Battle of Britain, squadron leader Peter Townsend later wrote:

If the Battle's full significance was not yet realized, it was clear enough that Dowding and Park had gained a unique, decisive victory.

Despite Churchill's brave speech, Hitler still thought that England might sue for peace. He wanted, if possible, to avoid the high cost of an invasion. He hoped that Germany's position of strength would sway British opinion and suggest to the enemy the wisdom of a negotiated peace. Through King Gustavus V of Sweden, Hitler had indicated that all he wanted from London was a free hand in Europe to pursue his *Lebensraum* policy. Hitler was prepared to stop his war against England if England would agree not to interfere with further German expansion on the Continent. How could London refuse such a generous offer? Yet, so far, the stubborn Englanders had shown no sign of accepting these terms. Hitler knew that a long-postponed invasion would be unwise. The Channel weather would turn nasty in the fall, ruling out all thoughts of an invasion. Any such delay could only favor the enemy by allowing Britons almost another year to recover from their losses on the mainland in France and Belgium—another year in which to grow stronger. Clearly, Hitler must decide soon.

Still . . .

While Hitler continued to hesitate, Churchill was drafting a strong reply to Hitler's peace proposal through the king of Sweden: "Before any such requests or proposals [for a peace settlement] could even be considered, it would be necessary that effective guarantees by deeds, not words, should be forthcoming from Germany which would ensure the restoration of a free and independent Czechoslovakia, Poland, Norway, Denmark, Holland, Belgium and above all, France."

In other words, England would not think of talking peace unless Hitler first put Europe back the way it was before his first aggressive acts of 1938. Churchill wrote as if he had Hitler right where he wanted him. Nothing could have been further from the truth. But if the plucky prime minister wanted to stir things up on the other side of the Channel, he succeeded. An angry and disappointed Hitler called for a meeting of his General Staff to discuss invasion plans. At the same time, Field Marshal General Hermann Göring, who was commander in chief of the Luftwaffe and second only to Hitler in the Nazi Party, issued an order outlining the "General Direction for the Operation of the Luftwaffe Against England." Scattered bombing attacks over Britain commenced at once. And the resolute Britons braced themselves for far worse to come.

Operation Sea Lion

Hitler met with his General Staff on June 30 at Kneibis in the Black Forest, some two hundred miles from the Channel area. At the meeting, code-named Tannenberg, Hitler consulted with his top advisers on how to proceed with the war against England.

Present at Tannenberg was General Alfred Jodl, chief of op-

Hitler and other top leaders study a report during World War II. Hitler's precipitous invasion of France left the leader a bit behind in his planning—he pondered several different plans for invading England.

erations at the German armed services' High Command. Jodl stood in awe of Hitler and held the almost fanatic belief that the national leader, the *Führer*, was a genius. At Hitler's request for ideas on what to do next, Jodl had submitted a paper entitled "The Continuation of the War Against England." Its proposals included a stepped-up air and sea war against British shipping, storage depots, factories, and the RAF; "terror attacks against the centers of population"; and "a landing of troops with the objective of occupying England."

Jodl felt that an invasion should be attempted only after control of the air had been established. He said that a landing would "finish off a country economically paralyzed and practically incapable of fighting in the air, if this is still necessary." He perhaps hoped, as did Hitler, that an invasion would not be needed.

On July 2, after "that gangster Churchill" had turned away Germany's invitation to surrender, Hitler said that he "could not conceive of anyone in England still seriously believing in victory." Yet the High Command still had done nothing about continuing the war with Britain. The following day, the High Command issued its first directive to the German armed services on the subject:

A Lion Without Claws?

Historians still wonder just how serious Hitler really was about invading England. The Führer delayed his decision several times to proceed with Operation Sea Lion, clinging to the hope that Britain would seek a peace settlement. The continual delays convinced many high-ranking German officers that Hitler had never really wanted to invade England. Interestingly, one officer who held that opinion was the general appointed by Hitler to command the invasion force.

Field Marshal Gerd von Rundstedt told Allied authorities after the war:

> The proposed invasion of England was nonsense, because adequate ships were not available. We looked upon the whole thing as sort of a game because it was obvious that no invasion was possible when our Navy was in no position to cover a crossing of the Channel or carry reinforcements. Nor was the German Air Force capable of taking on these functions if the Navy failed. I was always very skeptical about the whole affair. I have a feeling that the Führer never really wanted to invade England. He never had sufficient courage. He definitely hoped that the English would make peace.

(Top) Hermann Göring was commander and chief of the Luftwaffe, Germany's air force, and the one assigned to carry out the strategic bombardment of England. (Bottom) General Hugo Sperrle would command Luftwaffe forces from Belgium and Denmark.

The Führer and Supreme Commander has decided:

That a landing in England is possible, providing that air superiority can be attained and certain other necessary conditions fulfilled. The date of commencement is still undecided. All preparations to be begun immediately.

All preparations must be undertaken on the basis that the invasion is still only a plan, and has not yet been decided upon.

Clearly Hitler had not yet made a firm commitment to invade England. He would wait to see the effects of an all-out air assault on Britain by Göring's forces, the Luftwaffe. Serious preparations began at once, however, for the eventual execution of an invasion plan that loosely incorporated Jodl's earlier suggestions. The invasion plan from then on was known as Operation Sea Lion.

The Attackers

For Sea Lion to work, control of the sea was essential. But the British navy still owned the sea, almost unopposed by Hitler's small naval forces. The task of neutralizing the Royal Navy by either driving British ships out of the Channel or sinking them by bombing therefore fell to the Luftwaffe. Since Göring's pilots could hardly expect the cooperation of the Royal Air Force, it followed that the Luftwaffe must first eliminate the RAF as a factor. Göring more than willingly accepted responsibility for the rather formidable task. The boastful Göring in fact believed it would be easy. In a conference with high Luftwaffe commanders held in The Hague, Göring declared:

The enemy is already morally defeated. Our first objective will be the destruction of his fighter forces, partly in the air and partly on the ground, together with the destruction of his airfields. This objective will be attained within two or three days.

Göring then moved quickly to make good on his boasts. He gathered a force of thirteen hundred bombers to bomb vital British targets and the same number of fighters to protect the bombers from enemy fighters. Separating his planes into three Air Fleets—small, balanced, self-contained air forces—he assigned command of Air Fleet 2 to Field Marshal General Albert Kesselring, operating from air bases in northern France; 3 to Field Marshal General Hugo Sperrle, flying out of Dutch and Belgian fields; and 5 to Colonel General Hans-Jürgen Stumpf, who was based in Norway and had mostly bombers.

During the first phase of the Battle of Britain, the Germans planned to use strafing attacks on British seaports, Channel shipping, and airfields. Göring hoped that by attacking these targets he could coax the RAF into the air. He felt supremely confident that once the Luftwaffe was able to attack the RAF in the air, the superior quality and numbers of German aircraft and pilots would make short work of the Britons.

Day One

In the predawn hours of Wednesday morning, July 10, 1940, a heavy rain whipped across much of England from the North Atlantic. As dawn approached, the rain slacked off and gave way to showers. Towering cloud formations swirled high into the air and broke up, providing protective cover for Luftwaffe observation planes. A lone British Spitfire patrolling out of Coltishall fighter base spotted one such aircraft shortly after daybreak. The RAF pilot opened fire, but the German escaped into the thick, dark clouds. So began, in an incident mild and without decision, the Battle of Britain.

Scattered action involving RAF and Luftwaffe opponents over the Channel and above southeast Britain flared up here and there throughout the morning. Spitfires of No. 74 Squadron from Marston fighter base cut off a large enemy formation of Dornier Do 17 bombers, escorted by Messerschmitt Me 109 fighters. Flight Lieutenant Mungo Park drew first blood, sending a 109 crashing into the Channel with a three-second burst of his "Spit's" .303s. In the wild mix of twisting machines that followed, two 109s collided and

General Albert Kesselring was given command of Luftwaffe forces operating in northern France.

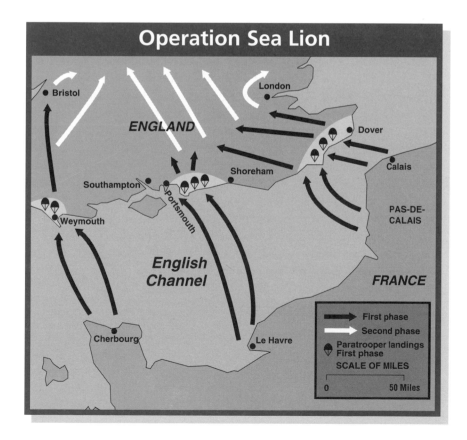

First Phase: The Battle Begins **21**

A German Messerschmitt 109 wings its way toward Britain.

went down, as well. Before breaking off, No. 74 Squadron dispatched a Dornier and damaged five more enemy aircraft.

Farther up the coast, German bombers attacked an unescorted convoy of British ships and sank one vessel. Hurricanes drove off the bombers, but more bombers took their place, this group with fighter escorts. Twenty Spitfires turned them away. Still Göring's black-topped, light-blue-bellied bombers and fighters came on. Spitfires from No. 43 Squadron confronted about thirty 109s near Margate. In a plunging attack, one RAF section leader locked onto the tail of a 109 and began firing at three hundred yards. He closed to fifty yards, all the while watching his bullets tear apart the Messerschmitt. "It just dropped out of the sky," he reported later. "What a thrilling sight!" The No. 43 pilots shot down two more enemy aircraft, destroying a total of three, while damaging several others before the clash ended. The morning's aerial activities, though busy, so far had not hinted of what Göring had in mind for the afternoon.

An Afternoon Affair

At about 1300, Colonel Johannes Fink answered the telephone in the converted bus that served as his headquarters at Cape Gris Nez airfield, between Calais and Boulogne, France. Fink held the position of *Kanakafu*, or "leader of the battle over the Channel," making him field commander over all Luftwaffe operations in the

English Channel area. An hour later, as a result of that phone call, seventy German aircraft took to the air from airfields in France and headed across the Channel.

Twenty Dornier Do 17s of Major Fuch's Third Group of Bomber Unit 2, climbed out of Arras–St. Léger airfield, southeast of Le Havre. Captain Hannes Trautloft led twenty Me 109s of the Third Group, Fighter Unit 51, from St. Omer, Belgium, and joined the 17s to fly close support. Completing the fighter escort were thirty twin-engined Me 110 fighters of Destroyer Unit 26, commanded by a one-legged officer, Major Huth.

At 1330, a British convoy, escorted by six No. 32 Squadron Hurricane fighters, from Biggin Hill fighter base near London, was steaming southwesterly through the Straits of Dover. At the same time, several radar stations began tracking the oncoming enemy aircraft over Calais. Elements from four other RAF Fighter Command squadrons were scrambled—rushed into the air—and sent winging off toward Dover.

Meanwhile, Lieutenant G.G.R. Bulmer, one of the Hurricane pilots, sighted the Germans and reported: "Waves of enemy bombers coming from the direction of France in boxes of six." For the next three minutes, six Hurricanes battled with seventy Luftwaffe aircraft. Then, suddenly, twenty-six Spitfires and Hurricanes appeared from out of the clouds to the north. The odds improved from six to thirty-two British fighters against seventy enemy fighters and bombers.

Me 109 commander Captain Hannes Trautloft, in a later report, said, "Suddenly the sky was full of British fighters. Today we were going to be in for a tough time." He was right.

(Above) A German bomber crew prepares to board their plane to take off across the English Channel. (Left) In a publicity shot from the movie The Battle of Britain, Nazi Heinkel bombers are harassed by RAF Spitfires.

Climbing in rapid spirals to a commanding height of fifteen thousand feet, the British fighter squadrons turned on their wings and plunged to the attack. Far below, standing on the beach near Dover, BBC reporter Charles Gardner watched the spectacular aerial display and recorded a description of it. Gardner shouted into his recorder over sounds of surf and hammering guns:

> There's one coming down in flames—there's somebody hit a German—and he's coming down—there's a long streak . . . Oh boy I've never seen anything so good as this—the RAF fighters have really got these boys taped!

The encounter ended at about 1400. Lost to the Luftwaffe were four aircraft, while the RAF had lost five. A small British ship was also sunk in the Channel. Other, lesser engagements continued throughout the balance of the day. In an action near Falmouth, a German bomber from Brittany sank a second British vessel.

That evening, Sir Edward Grigg, Britain's minister of information, described the afternoon affair to the House of Commons as "one of the greatest air battles of the war."

There could be little doubt that the Battle of Britain had begun. But despite the apparent enthusiasm of British observers, total wins and losses on the day hardly reflected a decisive RAF victory.

Hitler's Directives

Also on the same day, July 10, Hitler ordered all available artillery units moved into positions along the Channel to provide covering fire for an invasion fleet, already starting to gather in French, Dutch, and Belgian ports. And new gun emplacements were hastily constructed around Cape Gris Nez from Calais to Boulogne.

In anticipation of Operation Sea Lion, the proposed invasion of England across the Channel, Hitler placed gun emplacements on the coast of France.

In a July 13 letter to his closest ally, Italian dictator Benito Mussolini, Hitler declined the Fascist leader's offer to assist in the invasion of England. But Hitler's letter gave evidence that he was finally beginning to make up his mind. "I have made to Britain so many [peace] offers of agreement, even of cooperation, and have been treated so shabbily that I am now convinced that any new appeal to reason would meet with similar rejection. For in that country at present it is not reason that rules." Three days later, Hitler at last reached a decision.

On July 16, Hitler issued his now-famous "Directive No. 16 on the Preparation of a Landing Operation Against England," which stated:

Seek and Destroy

Commenting on the dogfight of July 10 that Sir Edward Grigg described as "one of the greatest air battles of the war," Squadron Leader Peter Townsend later wrote:

Thirty British single-seater fighters against twenty Me 109s. But it was nonsense to think the Me 109s were outnumbered. In addition to them were twenty Dorniers and thirty Me 110s, all part of a fighting force the British fighters had to oppose.

The Germans vainly believed that the Battle of Britain was going to be a romantic jousting contest in the clouds between the fighters of the RAF and of the Luftwaffe. But we RAF fighters were not in the least bit interested in the German fighters—except insofar as they were interested in us. Our job was defense. German fighters could do no harm to Britain. German bombers with their deadly loads were the menace. Our orders were to seek them out and destroy them. Only when their Me 109 escort interfered did it become a fleeting battle between fighter and fighter. But we tried to avoid them, not to challenge them.

The Me 110s were another matter. Long-range fighters with a tremendous forward firepower (twice that of the Me 109E), they were, however, highly vulnerable to Hurricanes and Spitfires, which could easily outmaneuver them and then have to face only a single machine gun firing rearward. Menaced by our single-seaters, the Me 110s immediately went into a "defensive circle," covering each other's tails, as they did that day.

German Me 109s on their way to England.

Since England, despite her militarily hopeless situation, still shows no sign of willingness to come to terms, I have decided to prepare a landing operation against England, and if necessary to carry it out.

The aim of this operation is to eliminate the English homeland as a base for the carrying on of the war against Germany, and, if it should become necessary, to occupy it completely.

It was now official. Preparations for Operation Sea Lion were scheduled for completion by mid-August.

On August 1, Hitler followed up with "Directive No. 17 for the Conduct of Air and Naval Warfare Against England." The directive's first order instructed the German air force "to overcome the English air forces with all means at its disposal and as soon as possible."

The Defenders

British air chief marshal Sir Hugh Dowding had spent much of his life shaping the RAF's Fighter Command into a force to be reckoned with. With the farsighted vision reserved for those destined for greatness, Sir Hugh had believed for years that an eventual confrontation between the RAF and the Luftwaffe over Britain was inevitable. And that long-prepared-for time of reckoning was at hand.

The fifty-eight-year-old Dowding, tall, lank, distant—some thought lonely—was a dedicated and determined career officer. He had been slated to retire in 1939 but was appointed to commander in chief of Fighter Command and extended in service until March 1940. On the next-to-last day of March, he was extended again until July 14, finally agreeing to remain until October. Thus, the defense of Britain resided with him. And his complex defense plan, which involved an array of widespread airfields and a web of early warning systems and communications networks, remained in place.

Dowding and Winston Churchill, however, had not seen eye to eye since the beginning, when Churchill had replaced Chamberlain as prime minister in May 1940. France, in the final stages of a desperate, losing battle for survival, was pleading for more help from the RAF. Although the French were continuing to resist, the fall of France was near. Churchill knew in his heart that it was too late to save France, but his great affection for the country moved him to want to help anyway. To members of Britain's War Cabinet who would make the final decision, Churchill proposed sending ten more fighter squadrons to France's aid. Dowding resisted strongly the suggestion that he commit his fighters to a losing cause when they were so desperately needed to defend England.

British air chief marshal Sir Hugh C.T. Dowding proved a brilliant strategist who had believed for years before World War II that the RAF would engage in battle with the Luftwaffe.

In the past four months alone, Fighter Command had lost fifteen squadrons in France, losses it could ill afford. Dowding argued that if Britain continued to aid France, there would be no fighters left to defend Britain. In a letter to Churchill, Dowding wrote:

> Once a decision has been reached as to the limits on which the Air Council and the Cabinet are prepared to stake the existence of the country, it should be made clear to the Allied Commanders on the Continent that not a single aeroplane from Fighter Command beyond the limit will be sent across the Channel no matter how desperate the situation may become.

Churchill, torn between wanting to help France and understanding the needs of Britain, finally, with great misgivings, supported Dowding's position. Dowding felt that Churchill ever after bore him a grudge for forcing a decision the prime minister had not wanted to make.

Within two weeks, Dowding's attempts to limit the role of Fighter Command in the Dunkirk evacuation brought him still more criticism. The air chief marshal, of course, wanted to render all possible assistance to the troops being forced off the Continent. At the same time, Dowding felt compelled to hold some squadrons in reserve for the coming defense of England. Dowding's choices were painful, but he felt that his first duty lay at home. He made his point clearly in a letter to the Air Council Staff, which governed all RAF operations and answered to the War Cabinet.

"I earnestly beg that my commitments [in Europe] be limited as far as possible," he wrote, "unless it is the intention of the Government to surrender the country in the event of a decisive defeat in France." His point was well taken.

Beyond Exhaustion

What often goes unmentioned was that Fighter Command flew 2,739 sorties during the Dunkirk evacuation. The RAF pilots flew beyond exhaustion, then flew some more. Much of the air action was screened from those on the ground by thick smoke and low cloud cover. Much more of the action occurred miles away from Dunkirk, as British pilots tried to prevent the Germans from reaching the battle scene. Because much of the RAF's contribution to the evacuation went unseen (thus unreported) at the beaches, soldiers and civilians alike criticized the RAF for not doing enough. They did not realize that an attempt by the RAF to do more than it had in fact accomplished might have left England defenseless.

In sum, the RAF lost 106 fighters, and 75 pilots were killed or captured after being shot down. But to avoid giving Germany information about British air strength, the figures could not be made public at the time.

"It Was a Great Hour"

Three RAF fighter pilots remember the days of Britain's summertime struggle for survival after the Battle of Britain.

"Above all, the thing that remains most clearly imprinted in my memory is the spirit which then existed," one flight lieutenant said, "the same spirit which inspired everybody from the Station Commander to the lowest aircraft-hand. For that was the first trial, the first flush of battle, and it was a great hour."

Another English pilot recalled: "We always had a devil-may-care sort of happiness. Lying in the sun waiting at readiness, there were moments of great beauty; the colors in the fields seemed brightest and the sky the deepest blue just before taking off for a big blitz. At dusk everything became peaceful. We were all happy at the thought of another day accomplished, our Hurricanes standing silhouetted against the sky, looking strong and confident, the darkness hiding their patched-up paintwork. In the morning whilst it was still dark, the roar of the engines being tested woke us for another day's work."

"They were wonderful, weird, exciting days," a squadron leader remembered. "Days when aircraft left beautiful curving vapor trails high in the sky, days when some of our friends took off and never came back, when others came back maimed and burnt, never to fight again."

In his face-off with the formidable forces of the Luftwaffe, Dowding could assemble only 650 fighters. Those he spread thinly across 52 squadrons at some 53 separate airfields. For maximum control and efficiency, he split Fighter Command into four groups, numbered 10 through 13. Each group was assigned a sector of the island to defend: southwestern, southeastern, central, and northern Britain, respectively. (In the early going, Dowding operated with three groups, but soon he recognized the need for a fourth, No. 10 Group, to defend the southwest sector.) Of these Fighter Command groups, No. 11 and No. 12 were the most important in that the Luftwaffe focused most of its attention on central and southeast England.

Air Vice Marshal Keith Park—Dowding's former senior air staff officer—commanded No. 11 Group, while Air Vice Marshal Trafford Leigh-Mallory headed No. 12 Group. Dowding's appointment of Park to lead No. 11 Group, a highly sought-after position, caused a bit of a stir within Fighter Command. When the opening occurred in 1940, Leigh-Mallory appeared to be the most likely choice for the job. He had already commanded No. 12 Group for three years. But Dowding decided to leave Leigh-Mallory in place and appointed Park instead.

Dowding's move did little to foster smooth relations within his organization, the success of which so depended on cooperation among all four groups. Leigh-Mallory never forgot or forgave his superior's slight. He later told Park that he would one day see Dowding sacked.

(Above) A British plane comes down over England—a loss the British could ill afford. In a controversial move, Dowding picked Air Vice Marshal Keith Park (right) to lead Britain's No. 11 Group over Air Vice Marshal Trafford Leigh-Mallory (far right), who, by rank, should have had the position.

During the storm and stress of future conflict, Dowding would count Park's enormous loyalty and respect among his blessings. For envy and discord, he could rely on Leigh-Mallory. In such troubled air did Dowding commence the defense of England.

The RAF Perseveres

Through the remainder of July, Göring continued a strategy of bombing and strafing attacks, concentrating principally on seaports and Channel shipping. By July 25, Johannes Fink, the Luftwaffe *Kanakafu*, had managed to drive British shipping out of the Channel. But at great cost. Fighter Command pilots had emphatically ended the myth of the fearsome Junkers Ju 87—the Luftwaffe's famous gull-winged dive-bomber, better known as the "Stuka." Although very effective against less-challenging defenders over Europe, the Stuka craft became easy pickings for the well-disciplined Spitfire and Hurricane pilots of Fighter Command. As Adolf Galland, Germany's great fighter-general, later pointed out:

> The slow speed of the Ju 87 turned out to be a great drawback. Owing to the speed-reducing effect of the externally suspended bombload, she reached only 150 m.p.h. when diving, and as the required altitude was between 10,000 and 15,000 feet, the Stukas attracted Spitfires and Hurricanes as honey attracts flies. The Stukas, once they peeled out of formation to dive singly on to their targets, were practically defenseless.

Another Luftwaffe aircraft that fell far short of German expectations was the twin-engined Messerschmitt Me 110 fighter. Under-armed and sluggish, the 110s could not match the firepower and maneuverability of Britain's Hurricanes and Spitfires. Against the eight-gun British fighters, they could survive only by forming a defensive ring and protecting one another's tails. Thus engaged in their own defense, the 110s could hardly render aid to the slower bombers assigned to their protective care. Along with the Stukas, the 110s added greatly to mounting Luftwaffe losses. The disappointing performance of the 110s in their roles as fighter escorts resulted in placing increased demands on already overworked Me 109 fighter squadrons. Their losses also began to climb alarmingly.

At the same time, British aircraft production increased sharply under the dynamic leadership of William Maxwell Aitken, Lord Beaverbrook. With

The Junker Ju 87, better known as the Stuka, turned out to be a big disappointment to the Germans. The Stuka's slow speed left it vulnerable to the RAF's experienced pilots.

The British had two distinct advantages over the Germans at the start of the Battle of Britain. (Above) William Maxwell Aitken, Lord Beaverbrook, minister of aircraft production, did a superior job of repairing and producing aircraft for the RAF. (Right) The British also used the new technology of radar to track the enemy before they could see them—a technology the Germans decided was too useless to develop.

Beaverbrook serving as minister of aircraft production, the number of fighters available to Dowding rose from 331 at the start of June to 600 a month later. From May through August—the height of what was called "the Beaver's" war effort—aircraft workers produced 1,875 fighters and repaired 1,872 others. The effort was lifesaving to Fighter Command.

Dowding reported later: "I saw my reserves slipping away like sand in an hour glass. Without his [Beaverbrook's] drive behind me I could not have carried on the battle."

On into August, Dowding's Fighter Command continued to repulse enemy efforts to destroy it. By detecting and tracking the locations of enemy aircraft, Britain's newly developed radar technology enabled Dowding to concentrate his fighters in greater numbers where needed most. Thus, by carefully limiting where and in what strength he used his fighters, as he had done in the battle of France and at Dunkirk, Dowding maintained a decided edge in the won-lost department. Göring answered Dowding by adding more and more aircraft to his ever-increasing day and night attacks. The number of German sorties—a sortie being a single flight by a single plane—reached 1,485 by August 8. Many aircraft flew several sorties in one day. The number of German sorties climbed higher each day. And still the RAF persevered.

Göring had by then recognized that his Luftwaffe couldn't sustain its increasing loss ratio indefinitely. Something had to be done right away. But what?

CHAPTER TWO

August Overture:
Luftwaffe Warm-Up

The Luftwaffe's limited attacks on British seaports and Channel shipping had failed to deal the hoped-for death blow to the RAF. Not unmindful of his responsibility to neutralize the British air force, and eager to look good in the eyes of his Führer, Göring decided to introduce stronger measures. To that purpose, he called his senior officers together at Karinhall, his comfortable headquarters outside Berlin. On August 6, 1940, there was a meeting to discuss stepping up the action over Britain.

"Attack of the Eagles"

Assembling to hear Göring outline his latest strategy for eliminating the RAF were Luftwaffe inspector general Field Marshal Erhard Milch, Air Fleet leaders Hans-Jürgen Stumpf and Hugo Sperrle, and other top air leaders. Out of that meeting came a bold plan called *Adlerangriff,* or "attack of the eagles." By means of this plan, Göring intended to keep his earlier promise to abolish RAF fighter opposition in southeast England in a matter of days. He further promised to achieve air mastery over all of Britain within a month.

In his estimates, Göring assumed good flying weather. He must have also assumed the inability of the RAF to strongly resist. In neither case did he assume correctly, as he set the starting date for an all-out assault on the RAF as August 13.

He called it *Adler Tag,* or Eagle Day.

While Göring prepared to eliminate the RAF once and for all, planning for Operation Sea Lion moved forward, although not without problems. Constant bickering amongst his General Staff must have caused Hitler to wonder whether they would ever agree on an invasion plan. The Wehrmacht leaders proposed multiple landings spread along 185 miles of English coastline. The German navy commanders insisted on a narrower front, maintaining that they could not supply enough vessels to operate on so broad a front. Nor could they adequately convoy invasion craft so thinly spread. Hitler finally effected a compromise by reducing the coastal area to 75 miles and assigning three armies to assault the beaches. He intended to be ready when the Luftwaffe cleared the skies.

Action over the Channel

On August 8, a British convoy of twenty-five merchant ships, escorted by two antiaircraft destroyers, eased into the Straits of Dover under cover of dark. The ships were carrying much-needed supplies to England. The Luftwaffe began preparing for *Adler Tag* by attacking the convoy in its largest force to date.

At about 0900, an initial attack wave of Stukas and Me 109s was beaten off by six RAF squadrons. Squadron Leader J.R.A. Peel, of Hurricane Squadron No. 145, reported his part in the action: "The enemy fighters, who were painted silver, were half-rolling and diving and zooming in climbing turns. I fired two five-second bursts at one and saw it dive into the sea. Then I followed another up in a zoom and got him as he stalled."

A German Stuka drops its load over the English Channel onto the British ships below.

The group flurry shifted southward over the sea. More fluttering aircraft of both sides splashed into the Channel. Then slugs from a trailing Messerschmitt ripped into Peel's Hurricane and it flipped forward, belching smoke. Peel went in for a bath. But his squadron mates circled overhead until a rescue boat reached him.

Action resumed at 1130, when about sixty more Stukas and three times as many 109s darkened the skies over the convoy. Hurricane Pilot Officer J.L. Crisp of Squadron 43 arrived on the scene and tore into a cluster of 109s. Already a survivor of several skirmishes and a crash landing, Crisp had soloed for the first time barely a year before. That he fought both fear and superior numbers was affirmed by the later entry in his pilot's log: "Met large quantities of assorted Hun A/Cs over convoys off I[sle] of Wight, fired at some, no certs [sure hits]. (Very scared.)"

The German bombers scored hits on a pair of ships and set them ablaze before being driven away by British fighters. But at 1615 the determined Luftwaffe struck at the convoy again with at least 130 aircraft of different types. Again Hurricanes and Spitfires met the Luftwaffe head-on. But the RAF fighters were too few to prevent the sinking of four ships and the damaging of six more.

The next day, August 9, a report to the British War Cabinet from Chief of the Air Staff Sir Cyril Louis Norton Newell stated that the fighting off the Isle of Wight represented the "biggest air action which has so far taken place off our coast. The enemy's main effort had developed into three successive attacks, involving at least 300 aircraft. . . . Our fighters had achieved great success." After reconciling initially exaggerated British claims (estimates on both sides were almost always high owing to reporting and accounting difficulties), the day's final loss tally was arrived at: about thirty-one German and nineteen RAF aircraft. Two RAF pilots were killed and another was wounded; thirteen were reported missing.

The weather closed off most of the air activities for the day. Still, losses for August 9 came in at five German aircraft destroyed, with the RAF losing four. August 10 saw a lone German Dornier Do 17 bomb West Malling fighter station, causing slight injuries to a few airfield ground workers. The Luftwaffe picked up the pace again on August 11.

"Sailor's August Eleventh"

At 0800 on a clear Sunday morning, Flight Lieutenant Adolphus "Sailor" Malan, a South African flying for the RAF, led his No. 74 "Tiger" Squadron Spitfires on a patrol toward Dover. Squadron members would later refer to the day as "Sailor's August Eleventh." Malan, in his words, "surprised eight Me 109s at 20,000 feet flying in pairs, staggered line astern towards Dover." As Malan and his mates rushed to greet the Germans, more 109s dived to aid their comrades. The sky turned busy with wildly darting, whirling warbirds trying to kill one another. Malan shot one German out of the air, while his squadron racked up seven others.

About an hour later, after a brief scuffle with two more

German bombers attack British air installations in southern England.

Me 109s, Malan barely escaped with his whiskers: "Eight Me 109s, who had previously escaped my attention, dived towards me and I climbed in [a] right-hand spiral, and they made no attempt to follow me." The 109s might have been low on fuel. Their small fuel tanks and long distances from home airfields allowed them only about ten minutes over target areas.

At about 1300, twenty-four Messerschmitt 110s appeared over a British convoy off Norfolk. They belonged to Test Group 210, an experimental group formed to test new equipment and battle tactics. The group, based at Calais-Marck airfield, was commanded by Captain Walter Rubensdörffer.

The 110s had been modified for use as fighter-bombers by making it possible for them to carry 500- and 1,000-pound bombs. Rubensdörffer had long thought of using the 110s in a dual role to make up for Germany's shortage of long-range bombers. If the experiment worked, the 110s could perform as bombers, then defend themselves without need of 109s flying escort. This would permit the 109s to focus on eliminating Fighter Command's Hurricanes and Spitfires. Many Luftwaffe pilots, including Adolf Galland, frowned on the idea, however.

Of the experiment, Galland wrote: "We fighter pilots looked upon this violation of our aircraft with great bitterness. To use a fighter as a fighter-bomber when the strength of the fighter arm is inadequate to achieve air superiority is putting the cart before the horse." But at first it looked as if it might work.

Rubensdörffer's 210 Group dived on the convoy and delivered their bombs, crippling two ships in the stream. Then, turn-

(Below) Flight Lieutenant Adolphus "Sailor" Malan. An exceptional commander, Malan's final victory score totaled thirty-five. (Below, right) A German pilots a Heinkel 115 and looks for a British target.

ing back into fighters, they fought off attacking Spitfires of Malan's No. 74 Squadron. All the 110s made it home safely. Two of Malan's pilots didn't. Rubensdörffer's group won the honors this day but would not fare so well in the near future.

Later that afternoon, No. 74 Squadron pilots did better. Pilot Officer Mackay Stephen described the encounter as

> a smasher. . . . A hell of a dog-fight. We found forty Me 110s in three groups, getting into position to attack a convoy. When the leader saw us approaching, he started forming into the Nazi's defensive formation circles. This suited us. Mungo Park, who was leading the formation, and his merry Tiger boys carried out Sailor's diving-in-and-out-of-the-circle tactics. Nazis were tumbling into the Channel one after another. Ten went for certain.

Still the day wore on for 74 Squadron. At 1600, Malan led his pilots aloft one more time, himself bagging another Me 109 over Folkestone. By the end of "Sailor's August Eleventh," Luftwaffe aircraft losses totaled thirty-eight against twenty-eight for the RAF.

August 12, Morning

August 12 continued in similar fashion only more so. Early that morning, Göring confirmed to his Air Fleet commanders that Eagle Day would commence the next day. German pilots were already heading across the Channel. In a series of punishing blows, the Luftwaffe struck the British naval base at Portsmouth, the Fighter Command airfields at Manston, Lympne, and Hawkinge, and five principal radar stations on the south coast.

At 0930, Luftwaffe major Outzmann's bomber group of Dornier Do 17 "Flying Pencils," so called because of their long, slender bodies, hammered home the first blow. The 17s dumped a string of 100-pound bombs on the runway and hangars at the coastal airfield of Lympne. Luftwaffe bombers returned later in the day. A total of 383 bombs were dropped to render the airfield unusable.

An hour later, Rubensdörffer's Group 210 set a northwest course over the Channel from Calais-Marck. The experimental group had been ordered to permanently destroy British coastal radar sites prior to Eagle Day. Their orders came directly from General Wolfgang Martini, commanding general of German signals and radar.

Over his radio telephone (R/T) at 1100, Rubensdörffer ordered Flight Lieutenant Otto Hintze to "Proceed on special mission," adding, "Good hunting." Eight 109s of Hintze's No. 3 *Staffel* (a flight element usually made up of nine aircraft) swung east toward Dover. Rubensdörffer then split the remaining 110s of his 210 Group. Flight Lieutenant Martin Lutz's section angled off toward Pevensey, while Flight Lieutenant Wilhelm Roessiger led another

Radio Detection And Ranging

Perhaps the least-known hero of the Battle of Britain was Robert Watson-Watt, the father of British radar.

RADAR, a system for Radio Detection And Ranging, provided the British with the ability to "see" approaching enemy aircraft in advance of their arrival over England. Radio waves transmitted toward Europe would reflect or "bounce" off an aircraft in a transmission path within a 120-mile range. A reflection appearing in the form of a trace or "blip" would then appear on the graduated scale of a radar screen. The blip would fix the aircraft's position at point of contact. From there, a radar operator could plot the aircraft's course, speed, and estimated time of arrival.

This information was then relayed to the "filter room" at Fighter Command headquarters in Bentley Priory, near Stanmore. The filter room served as clearinghouse for all incoming radar plots originating from some fifty-one (at the time of the battle's beginning) radar stations strung along Britain's coast. Most stations, with their tall, spindly masts, were located in the southeastern counties opposite France.

In the filter room, WAAF plotters, using battery-powered electromagnetic rakes, moved colored markers across a large-scale gridded map of the British Isles and its surroundings. This plot information was updated every five minutes. From a balcony above the plotting table, a controller passed on information that had been filtered and classified to the Fighter Command operations room located next door. Intercept information was then relayed to Fighter Command sector stations for further communication to all affected airfields to "scramble" their pilots and aircraft. More often than not, arriving enemy aircraft would find Hurricanes and Spitfires already alerted and enjoying a height advantage.

The Germans failed to grasp how important the British radar network was to the successful defense of Britain. Since the Nazis had tried and failed to develop an efficient radar system of their own, they arrogantly assumed that the British, too, would fail. But, then, they didn't know Robert Watson-Watt.

An early model antenna stands guard to warn England of approaching aircraft. At the start of the Battle of Britain, Göring placed a high priority on attacking radar installations. When this strategy proved costly, Göring called off the attacks, deeply underestimating the advantages of the system.

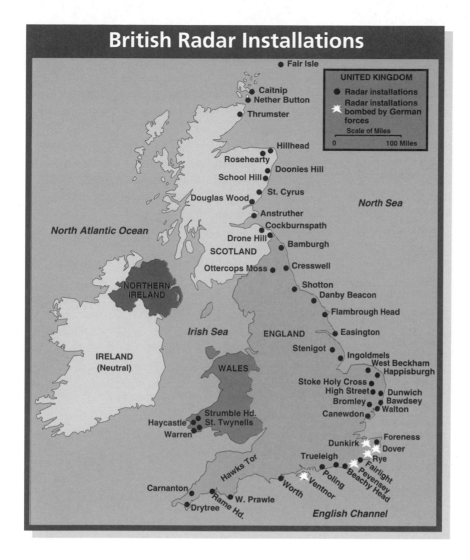

British Radar Installations

UNITED KINGDOM
● Radar installations
✱ Radar installations bombed by German forces

Scale of Miles
0   100 Miles

Fair Isle
Caitnip
Nether Button
Thrumster
Hillhead
Rosehearty
Doonies Hill
School Hill
St. Cyrus
Douglas Wood
Anstruther
Cockburnspath
Drone Hill
Bamburgh
SCOTLAND
Cresswell
Ottercops Moss
Shotton
Danby Beacon
Flambrough Head
Easington
ENGLAND
Stenigot
Ingoldmels
West Beckham
Happisburgh
Stoke Holy Cross
High Street
Dunwich
Bromley
Bawdsey
Canewdon
Walton
Foreness
Strumble Hd.
Haycastle
St. Twynells
Dunkirk
Dover
Warren
Trueleigh
Rye
Fairlight
Pevensey
Poling
Beachy Head
Carnanton
Worth
Ventnor
Hawks Tor
W. Prawle
Rame Hd.
Drytree
English Channel

North Sea
North Atlantic Ocean
NORTHERN IRELAND
Irish Sea
IRELAND (Neutral)
WALES

section toward Rye. Rubensdörffer's group of eight 110s proceeded on to Dunkirk.

At Dover, Hintze's pilots sighted the radar installation and dived to the attack. They exploded three bombs at the site, but failed to knock down the 350-foot radar masts. Constructed of steel and anchored in steel-reinforced concrete, the narrow towers defied destruction by anything less than a direct hit.

Meanwhile, Lutz's 110 pilots delivered eight 1,000-pound bombs at Pevensey, shattering transmitters and knocking out the station. They then continued on to unload their racks of 150-pound bombs on Manston airfield, arriving about 1330. The Germans caught all but one or two Spitfires of No. 65 Squadron on the ground.

Lutz reported: "The fighters were all lined up. Our bombs fell right amongst them."

More Messerschmitts followed Lutz's at Manston, dropping a total of 175 bombs and claiming direct hits on hangars and living

"An Essential Operational Factor"

Formed by Royal Warrant on June 28, 1939, the Women's Auxiliary Air Force, or WAAF, numbered fewer than two thousand women when war broke out in September of that year.

When Britain declared war on Germany, the BBC broadcast an immediate appeal for volunteers to expand the ranks of the WAAF. Women from every level of English life streamed into recruiting centers, responding to their country's call even before sufficient supplies of uniforms and equipment and adequate accommodations became available. Preparations for proper training and a code of conduct for women new to service life lagged behind enlistments, adding to the hardships faced by new recruits.

In the beginning, the RAF allowed women to serve only as cooks, motor transport drivers, equipment assistants, orderlies, or clerks. But deeper into the war, the job choices increased to seventy-five—not counting twenty-two officer commissions—and 182,000 women were employed. Without the WAAF, the RAF would have needed 150,000 more men.

Resented at first by some RAF members, who felt that the service held no place for women and that women might panic under fire, the WAAFs eventually won the admiration of their male comrades. Working alongside the RAF both at home and abroad, the WAAFs also won many awards and honors, including six Military Medals for "gallantry in the face of the enemy."

In gratitude, the British Air Council stated: "It is the view of the Air Council that an essential operational factor of the RAF would be missing if there was no WAAF."

A former RAF group captain and commander of a fighter station during the Battle of Britain agreed with the Air Council. "I had cause to thank goodness," he said, "that the country could produce such a race of women as the WAAF on my Station."

British Gunner Girls "man" a night action station during the Battle of Britain.

quarters. The German section leader also claimed four Hurricanes and five other aircraft destroyed on the ground. The airfield was all but eliminated for further use by Dowding's Fighter Command.

At Rye, WAAF (Women's Auxiliary Air Force) trackers watched on their radar screens as the blips of Roessiger's 110s approached straight at them. Bombs exploded outside, rocking the hut. A trace of blinding light flashed on the tube then faded to black.

WAAF corporal Daphne Carne described the scene outside:

> Huge clouds of earth and mud covered the platform of the transmitter tower. . . . The road was pitted with craters and great gaps were torn in the high steel railings enclosing the compound. Where the cook-house had been there was an enormous lake on which floated splintered planks of wood and all manner of kitchen utensils.

Such sights would soon become all too familiar.

All the main buildings were destroyed by 500- and 1,000-pound bombs, but radar station crews restored the site to active service in three and a half hours.

At Dunkirk, a 1,000-pound bomb courtesy of Rubensdörffer's group shook the concrete foundation of a radar transmitter, shifting it several inches. But damage was so slight that plotting at the station continued without interruption.

On the Isle of Wight, a fifth radar installation at Ventnor came under attack by seventy-eight Junkers Ju 88 dive-bombers and their fighter escorts. Their bombs inflicted severe damage, disabling the station for the next eleven days.

August 12, Afternoon

In midafternoon three separate formations of Dornier Do 215s and Junkers Ju 87s struck the airfield at Hawkinge. The dive-bombers damaged hangars and left the landing strip riddled with bomb craters.

By this time, dogfights filled the skies over southeast England. Throngs of civilians, Frances Faviell among them, gathered in the streets and meadows below to watch. Later Faviell would write:

> It seemed impossible at first to believe that these were actually deadly battles and not mock ones. It gave one a strange, shaking, sick feeling of excitement to watch their every movement. . . . Twisting, turning, their guns blazing, the sunlight picking them out in the clear sky, they would dive under, over, round, and then straight at their opponents until one would fall in a trail of smoke and flame, often with a gleaming parachute like a toy umbrella preceding the final crash to earth. It was horrible—but it had a macabre [morbid] fascination impossible to resist.

Meanwhile, another formation of determined Ju 88s plunged through a steel wall of flak at the Portsmouth naval base on the

German Junker Ju 88s head out over England.

south coast. Their bombs struck hard at the city and dock area. Fires in their wake burned far into the night.

The Luftwaffe's savage onslaught on Britain cost the Germans thirty-one machines that day. Britain's radar defenses, although damaged, remained on line. General Martini, who understood to some degree the importance of British radar, received the news with keen disappointment. But Göring and his other advisers failed to realize how vital the new technology of radar was to Britain's defense system. Göring's lack of understanding, coupled with the difficulties and dangers involved in the destruction of radar towers, led him to make one of his poorest decisions of the war.

"It is doubtful whether there is any point in continuing the attacks on radar sites," Göring said to his Air Fleet commanders three days later at his Karinhall headquarters, "in view of the fact that not one of them attacked has so far been put out of action." Only two more attacks were ever launched against British radar installations. As later events would show, Göring's failure to pursue the destruction of England's vital radar defenses was a major strategic mistake.

On August 12, in 732 sorties, British Fighter Command lost twenty-two valuable aircraft. The Luftwaffe appeared to be warming to its task. And the next day was *Adler Tag*—Eagle Day!

CHAPTER THREE

August 13–15: Three Days of the Eagle

A drizzling rain and low clouds settled over the Luftwaffe bomber bases in northern France on the long-awaited morning of August 13. On Eagle Day, all three of Göring's Air Fleets stood poised and ready for an early strike on Britain. Hermann Göring had promised to eliminate the RAF in southeast England in four days, *assuming* fair weather. But even the high-ranking marshal of the reich could not command the weather, and Göring was forced to postpone the first raids until afternoon. The command communications system somehow broke down, however, and his orders didn't filter through the network fast enough to reach all units.

Seventy-four Dornier Do 17 bombers of Bomber Unit 2 took off from Arras–St. Léger airfield in France at 0550 and headed for Eastchurch airfield on the Isle of Sheppey in the Thames Estuary without a fighter escort. Aided by thick cloud cover, the Dorniers, led by Colonel Johannes Fink, arrived over target safely. At 0702, they commenced bombing what they thought was an important airfield belonging to Keith Park's No. 11 group in Fighter Command's southeast sector. In reality, Fink had received faulty information from German intelligence operations, and his target was a Coastal Command light-bomber station of lesser importance. Fink's raiders caught two visiting fighter squadrons on the ground, but the fighters escaped the bombing without harm.

Chief Air Marshal Dowding had been forewarned by England's priceless radar system that Colonel Fink's Dorniers were approaching Eastchurch. In keeping with his policy of concentrating flexible units where most needed, Dowding directed Hurricane No. 111

Hurricanes of the Royal Air Force fly above the clouds. Dowding believed in keeping small, flexible units of squadrons and allowing pilots in the squadrons to decide how and when to attack.

Squadron to head off the Dorniers. The Hurricanes arrived just as the unescorted bombers were finishing their runs. Set upon by Hurricanes of No. 111 Squadron, the Dorniers dodged into the clouds and raced toward home. Hurricanes from No. 151 Squadron and Spitfires from Sailor Malan's No. 74 joined in the chase that followed.

In the first air action of the day, the RAF fighters knocked down four Dorniers. Only by a small miracle did four other badly damaged Dorniers manage to limp home. German bombs caused little damage at the Eastchurch field, interrupting RAF operations for barely ten hours. The day's next action occurred near Odiham.

A formation of Ju 88s of Bomber Unit 54—another unit that had missed Göring's orders to cancel the morning raids—was proceeding toward assigned targets at Odiham airfield and the Royal Aircraft Factory at Farnborough. They were suddenly distracted by Hurricanes and Spitfires of three squadrons: Nos. 43, 601, and 64. Badly rattled, the 88s missed their targets, wildly scattering their bombs about the countryside before departing quickly.

The fighters then turned their attention to a new threat, as described by Pilot Officer Mayers of 601 Squadron:

We saw about twenty-four Ju 88s [part of Unit 54] escorted by many Me 110 and 109s. The fighters were stepped up into the sun [flying one above another in a diagonal line]. We flew alongside the bombers on the left until we were slightly ahead. I started to attack the bombers, but as the [German] escort came down in a dive I made a climbing right turn into the 110s. I saw part of the roof and fuselage of one 110 break away as I fired one burst of about three seconds from head on. The enemy aircraft continued in a dive but I didn't see what happened to it.

Despite help from their fighter escorts, the bombers were turned back before reaching their targets. Flying Officer J.L. Crisp of 43 Squadron, who also took part in the engagement, later wrote a brief description in his logbook: "Met fifty Ju 88s and Me 110s, fired on one 88 and two 110s. Good party."

By 0930, the Luftwaffe had launched five major attacks on southern England. So far, Göring's "eagles" had enjoyed little success.

Tuesday Matinee

After a brief lull in the action, phones started ringing again shortly after noon in Fighter Command ready rooms, where pilots awaited a call to action. RAF pilots resumed their scrambles all over southern England, as the Luftwaffe continued to darken Britain's skies with aircraft. With clearing weather conditions, Göring directed waves of Ju 88s and Ju 87 Stukas, and their escorting 109s and 110s, toward targets at Southampton, Middle Wallop, Detling, and Rochford.

While 110s fought off RAF fighters, a flock of Ju 88s broke through British defenses to successfully bomb warehouses and set the docks afire. But six 110s went down before RAF guns. A group of Stukas tried to move inland to attack Middle Wallop but met a waiting band of Spitfires from 609 Squadron. The Stukas left in great haste, scattering their bombs across three counties. The wreckage of nine Stukas, victims of the 609 pilots, added to the growing aircraft litter spread across those same counties.

General Alan Brooke, recent commander of the BEF's Second Corps at Dunkirk, witnessed the Stuka slaughter from the ground near Portland with Winston Churchill and others.

British general Sir Alan Brooke watched the heavy fighting over southern England.

Baker's Dozen

Thirteen Spitfires from 609 Squadron entertained sixty German raiders at teatime (1600) on Eagle Day.

"We took off, thirteen machines in all," Pilot Officer David Crook wrote, "with the CO leading, and climbed up over Weymouth. After a few minutes I began to hear a German voice talking on the R/T, faintly at first and then growing in volume. By a curious chance this German raid had a wave-length almost identical with our own and the voice we heard was that of the German Commander talking to his formation as they approached us across the Channel."

The German formation of about sixty aircraft arrived over Weymouth about fifteen minutes later. Included in the formation were Ju 87 dive-bombers with 109 fighter escorts, and, lagging about two miles behind, some Me 110s. The RAF squadron leader led his Spitfires through the 109s and attacked the Ju 87 formation. The fight was on! In the midst of the action, one RAF pilot saw five Stukas plunging down in flames. A Polish pilot named Novi shot down two 109s. Crook closed with another 109 and opened fire. The German fighter fell earthward trailing smoke.

"I followed him down for some way," Crook wrote, "and could not pull out of my dive in time to avoid going below the clouds myself. I found that I was about five miles north of Weymouth, and then I saw a great column of smoke rising from the ground. My Me 109 lay in a field, a tangled heap of wreckage burning fiercely, but with the black crosses on the wings still visible. I found out later that the pilot was still in the machine . . . I could see everybody streaming out of their houses and rushing to the spot."

The afternoon "tea" netted thirteen enemy machines destroyed with six more probables or damaged. All Spitfires returned safely to their field at Middle Wallop, one with a bullet hole through its wing.

He later wrote: "We found a German plane which had just come down. Pilot was all burned up, but as a 500-lb bomb was in the debris which was burning, we did not stop long." The Junkers Ju 87 Stukas, once dreaded in the face of little opposition over Europe, proved to be nearly helpless in actions against RAF Hurricanes and Spitfires. The Stuka would now become one of the most sought-after RAF targets.

More Stukas, flying in thick cloud cover, couldn't find the Fighter Command airfield at Rochford. The 87s were forced to dump their loads and run when jumped by Spitfires from 65 Squadron over Canterbury. But still another group of Ju 86 Stukas, with Major Gotthardt Handrick's Messerschmitts running interference, penetrated a ring of defending fighters at Detling to score the day's greatest success. The Coastal Command airfield absorbed heavy damage and its commanding officer was killed, as were a number of civilians who had been enjoying afternoon tea.

Spitfires of No. 65 Squadron take off to confront the Luftwaffe. On Eagle Day this squadron drove off an attack by the Stukas.

The air encounters went down with the sun. A few night attacks by Heinkel He 111 bombers added little more to the German credits for the day. In total, the Luftwaffe had launched 1,485 sorties—far fewer than Göring had intended—at the cost of 46 aircraft. The RAF, in countering with 700 sorties, lost 13 fighters in the air and one on the ground. The wings of the eagle had been, if not broken, bent badly. Eagle Day had failed.

A Furious Fifteenth

More poor weather prevented large-scale operations on August 14, and the Luftwaffe managed to mount only 489 sorties. The next day—a day to become more deserving of the *Adler Tag* title—the Luftwaffe sorties would more than triple. Göring decided to unleash the Luftwaffe's full fury on England, using all three of his Air Fleets together for the first—and last—time. And the RAF would have to use all four groups of Fighter Command to turn them back. But air activities started late.

Indeed, Göring canceled operations for a brief time because of continued heavy overcast, but used the downtime to call Field Marshals Kesselring and Sperrle, leaders of Air Fleets 2 and 3, to Karinhall for a strategy session. The Air Fleet commanders brought their staffs with them, leaving junior officers in charge. Word of canceled operations somehow failed to reach Air Fleet 2 until too late. When the weather cleared at about 1100, junior officers proceeded with the attack plan. The confusion that resulted because of orders being canceled and reinstated, much the same as on Eagle Day, upset the timing among the three German Air Fleets throughout the day. Units that failed to receive the cancellation orders left according to the original schedule. The remaining units departed according to revised schedules. What had been planned as a smoothly coordinated, well-timed attack turned into a catch-as-catch-can affair.

Air Fleet 2 Attacks

The first action on August 15 began at about 1130. Two Ju 87 Stuka groups assembled with their fighter escorts—Me 109s from Adolf Galland's Fighter Unit 26—over Calais. About sixty aircraft in all, they headed across the Straits of Dover and turned north near Dungeness. A squadron each of Hurricanes and Spitfires met the German formation, knocking down four Stukas. The remaining 87s got through to bomb the airfields at Lympne and Hawkinge. The hard-hit Lympne field was shut down for two full days; the more important base at Hawkinge sustained only minor damage. Galland added a Spitfire to his increasingly impressive score. The improving weather conditions had by then spurred new orders from Göring to proceed with a large-scale attack.

Air Fleet 5 Strikes from Stavanger

Colonel General Stumpf's Air Fleet 5 complied by launching two bomber groups to attack targets on Britain's northeast coast in the Newcastle and Sunderland area. One group left from Stavanger, Norway; the other from Aalborg, Denmark. Both groups left shortly before 1200 and flew on diagonal headings toward Northumberland and Yorkshire. Stumpf also sent twenty seaplanes ahead of his bombers to stage a mock attack in the Firth of Forth region and estuary north of Edinburgh, Scotland. He hoped to lure fighters from Fighter Command's Group No. 13, commanded by Air Vice Marshal Richard Ernest Saul, away from the main German attack force.

British radar began "blipping" a little after 1215. WAAF trackers reported twenty—later forty-plus—enemy aircraft approaching. Spitfires of 72 Squadron took to the air within fifteen minutes, hoping to intercept the Germans off the Farne Islands. They were soon joined by fighters scrambled from 605, 41, 79, and 607 Squadrons. The defenders then totaled about forty.

The bomber group from Stavanger mistakenly converged with the twenty seaplane decoys near the Firth of Forth. An error in navigation over the long distances involved—approximately 1,100 miles round-trip—had caused the bombers to reach Britain about seventy miles north of their intended destination. The raiding aircraft from Stavanger now numbered 118: the 20 seaplanes, 63 Heinkel He 111 bombers of Bomber Unit 26, and 35 Messerschmitt Me 110 fighters of Destroyer Unit 76. Pilots of Spitfire Squadron 72 from Acklington spotted them first. They reported a massed German bomber formation approaching in a reverse wedge at eighteen thousand feet, escorted by two waves of 110s flying about a thousand feet above.

One excited Spitfire pilot shouted over his radio: "There must be hundreds of them!" A slight exaggeration, but the Germans did outnumber the British about three to one.

Four Spitfires from 72 Squadron tackled the 110s, and the others attacked the bomber force. In the aerial free-for-all that followed, many of the Heinkels jettisoned their bombs and turned for home. Some of the hardier bomber pilots pressed on toward their targets. The bomber groups then split into two sections, one section aiming for RAF targets near Tyneside, the other heading south to other assigned targets.

Spitfires from 79 Squadron joined their 72 Squadron friends in attacking the Messerschmitts. The Germans, while admitting to losing six 110s, claimed the destruction of two Spitfires. In his combat report describing how he downed one of the Spitfires, a Messerschmitt pilot, Flight Sergeant Linke, wrote that he closed to within fifty yards of the Spitfire and "did some good deflection shooting. The Spitfire reared up, then spiralled vertically down." Then, diving to evade two Englishmen on his tail, Linke saw two Spitfires hit the water. RAF bullets riddled Linke's port engine, and he barely struggled back across the North Sea to Stavanger.

Another 110 pilot escaped death by an even narrower margin. Flight Sergeant Richter blacked out after being hit in the head by a Spitfire bullet. Richter slumped forward against the control stick, causing the Messerschmitt to nose over. Then the

(Above, left) The WAAF in a radar plotting room give the edge to British pilots by alerting them minutes before of German fighter and bomber positions. (Below) RAF Spitfires in attack formation move to defend England.

aircraft spun out of control and plunged toward the sea. Sergeant Geischecker, the backseat radio operator, apparently sure that his pilot was dead, bailed out over the North Sea. Richter came to in time to regain control and limp home in his damaged aircraft, but Geischecker was neither seen nor heard from again.

The most northerly bomber section, nagged constantly by RAF fighters, eventually dropped most of their bombs into the ocean and turned for home. The southerly bomber section inflicted slight damage on the coastal village of Seaham, and a few houses in Sunderland were destroyed. Neither section managed to find its intended targets, the airfields at Dishforth and Linton-upon-Ouse. Official British files show that Group No. 13 pilots shot down nineteen Me 110s and eight He 111s, without loss of a single RAF aircraft during the encounter.

Air Fleet 5 Attacks from Aalborg

About ninety miles farther south, fifty unescorted Junkers Ju 88s belonging to Bomber Unit 30 droned in toward Flamborough Head, near Bridlington on the east-central coast of England. (It was off Flamborough Head that Admiral John Paul Jones in the American ship *Bon Homme Richard* captured the British vessel *Serapis* in 1779.) The bombers, flying out of Aalborg, Denmark, formed the second attack wing of Stumpf's Air Fleet 5. British radar discovered their presence at the same time as Stumpf's northern wing. Their target, the airfield at Driffield, fell within the defensive area of Air Vice Marshal Leigh-Mallory's Group No. 12.

While the air battle continued in the north, Leigh-Mallory sent Spitfires from 616 Squadron and Hurricanes from 32 Squadron to deter the Ju 88s. The British fighters engaged the Luftwaffe bombers about five miles off the coast. In the running battle that followed, Leigh-Mallory's pilots shot down eight German bombers. The remaining bombers pressed on through the fighters to off-load their explosives at Driffield airfield, home of RAF Bomber Command's No. 4 group. Their bombs destroyed twelve Whitley bombers on the ground and riddled the runway with large craters. Four hangars and three groups of buildings were also demolished. More bombs were dropped at Bridlington, destroying some houses and striking an ammunition dump. RAF defenders, in older aircraft including Blenheims from Catterick and Defiants up from Kirton-in-Lindsey, finally chased the 88s back out to sea. On the day, Stumpf's Air Fleet 5 inflicted little damage on Britain while suffering the heavy loss of thirty-five German aircraft. The RAF lost none. Air Fleet 5 would never again schedule daylight operations over Britain.

Göring had hoped to draw British fighters away from the southeast sector by attacking in the north. Luftwaffe bombers would then meet with less resistance when they attacked more vital targets in the south. But Air Chief Marshal Sir Hugh Dowding refused to be decoyed and held fast to his defense plan.

Air Fleet 2 Attacks Again

Enemy aircraft belonging to Kesselring's Air Fleet 2 again approached England's coast shortly after 1400. Their targets lay in Essex, Suffolk, and north Kent. Air Vice Marshal Park sent seven squadrons aloft to greet them. Interceptions became difficult owing to the confused, scattered manner of the attacks. RAF pilots were routinely outnumbered and often poorly positioned, sometimes still trying to get off the ground when the bombing began.

Nine Hurricanes of No. 1 Squadron scrambled out of North Weald and clashed with a group of forty Me 109s and 110s about ten miles offshore from Harwich. The 110s belonged to Rubensdörffer's Test Group 210. While their 109 escorts held off No. 1 Squadron's Hurricanes, the 110s slipped inland to attack the airfield at Martlesham. The attack began at 1525 and ended five minutes later. Hurricanes from 17 Squadron, based at Martlesham, vectored back from patrol near the Thames Estuary, arrived too late, and found their field in smoking ruins. Rubensdörffer was already leading his 210 Group home to Calais, to rearm and refuel. He had led his pilots on another successful mission, but his luck was running out. In three hours, he would be dead.

While Rubensdörffer headed home, a large formation of about a hundred Dornier Do 17 bombers and still more Messerschmitt Me 109 fighters advanced on Kent, south of the Thames.

British air chief marshal Leigh-Mallory directed the RAF's Air Group 12 to victory. (Above) A squadron of high-speed Hurricanes patrols high above the British coastline. Each plane carried eight powerful machine guns to take on the heavier German bombers.

Four Fighter Command squadrons couldn't turn back the attackers. While the 109s took on the RAF fighters, the Dorniers moved through the air battles and bombed Eastchurch, Rochester, and Hawkinge, the latter for the second time that day.

Rochester was the hardest hit. Thirty Do 17s belonging to Bomber Unit 3 and led by Colonel von Chamier-Glisczinski showered 100-pound fragmentation bombs on the airfield below. Many of the bombs tore up the runway. Still more smashed into Short Brothers aircraft works, delaying for several months production of the RAF's long-range Stirling bombers.

Von Chamier-Glisczinski's combat report indicated: "Aero-engine works repeatedly hit. Copious [plentiful] flame and smoke."

The raid cost Air Fleet 2 five or six aircraft, but the RAF this time paid a higher price, losing nine fighters in the battle.

Air Fleet 3 Arrives Late

Suddenly, a hush fell over Britain. For nearly two hours, the Luftwaffe stayed home, allowing Fighter Command a much-needed break to rest its exhausted pilots and service its overworked aircraft. Field Marshal General Sperrle's Air Fleet 3 was slated to attack the island immediately following the withdrawal of Air Fleet 2. But Göring's orders that morning, first stopping then restarting operations, caused a timing gap in the German schedule. Consequently, the Luftwaffe missed a great chance to catch most of the RAF fighters on the ground.

When Air Fleet 3 finally got on track, it appeared in great strength over Britain. A massive force of Junkers Ju 88 and Ju 87 dive-bombers, escorted by Messerschmitt Me 109 and 110 fighters, made landfall at about 1720 and began spreading out over Hampshire and Wiltshire. Dowding met the waves of over two hundred German aircraft with his largest yet concentration of fighters. He dispatched six fighter squadrons and a section from Air Vice Marshal Sir Christopher Brand's No. 10 Group, and seven squadrons from Park's No. 11 Group. To the tune of chattering guns, shrieking engines, and exploding aircraft, the Luftwaffe and RAF pilots rocked and rolled across England's fair skies, locked in a deadly embrace.

Ju 88 squadron leader Captain Jochen Helbig shouted into his radio: "Spitfires to port . . . Fighter attack from astern. Am being attacked!"

Pilots relax between sorties. This proved a rare occasion for the pilots of the RAF, who often had to fly beyond exhaustion to compensate for their fewer numbers.

Then Helbig's radio operator–gunner Flight Sergeant Schlund reported on the intercom: "Spitfire astern and to starboard . . . 400 yards . . . 300 . . . 250." Schlund held fire until he could wait no longer, finally firing only an instant ahead of his enemy.

Helbig yanked the 88 to starboard. The Spitfire flashed by, its belly riddled with Schlund's bullets and its engine beginning to trail smoke. Helbig's 88 survived the fight, as did one other bomber from his group. Five others went down in as many minutes. In Helbig's group of fifteen bombers heading for the naval airfield at Worthy Down, only three reached their target.

The Luftwaffe suffered heavy losses everywhere. A few bombs were dumped on Portland, but most of the bombers jettisoned their loads and raced toward home. Twelve Ju 88s continued toward Middle Wallop, however, despite a curtain of defending fighters.

Spitfire pilot David Crook of 609 Squadron recalled:

> We got off only a few minutes before they arrived at the aerodrome and were unable to intercept them, or even to see them until they were practically over the aerodrome, as they dived out of the sun, dropped their bombs, and then streamed back towards the coast as hard as they could go.

The 88s struck two hangars and destroyed one plane on the ground, while damaging five others. "But we were attacking them the whole time," added Crook, "and shot down at least five."

Air Fleet 3 closed out their afternoon assault with losses totaling twenty-five aircraft: eight Ju 88s, four Ju 87s, and thirteen Me 109s. Fighter Command lost sixteen Spitfires and Hurricanes. Weary RAF pilots hoped at that point to secure operations for the day. But the Luftwaffe wasn't finished.

One More Time

Air Fleet 2 struck one more time. At 1810, radar reported waves of about a hundred enemy aircraft approaching. The latest raiders crossed the coast at Dungeness and set courses for No. 11 Group's sector station airfields at Redhill, Kenley, and Biggin Hill. Fighter Command's available squadrons were either on the ground refueling or in the air and needing to refuel soon. Dog-tired pilots from 601 Squadron, just completing a patrol and low on fuel, plunged to intercept the intruders. The leader of No. 11 Group, Keith Park, called over four squadrons from an eastern sector to help out. He would later commit more squadrons from his western flank.

At Park's Uxbridge headquarters, on the outskirts of London, Winston Churchill and General Hastings Ismay, the prime minister's representative on the Chiefs of Staff Committee, watched the tracking activities in the plotting room. Soon, a furious battle developed overhead. Ismay later wrote: "At one moment every single

A Summertime Swim

RAF pilot officer Stevenson of "Sailor" Malan's 74 Squadron engaged a dozen Me 109s over the Thames on Eagle Day. He hadn't planned on bobbing for sea bass, but that wasn't all that took his breath away that day.

> There were about twelve Me 109s diving at me from the sun and at least half of them must have been firing deflection shots at me. There was a popping noise and my control column became useless. I found myself doing a vertical dive, getting faster and faster. I pulled the hood back. I got my head out of the cockpit and the slipstream tore the rest of me clean out of the machine. My trouser leg and both shoes were torn off. I saw my machine crash into the sea a mile off Deal. It took me twenty minutes to come down. I had drifted eleven miles out to sea. One string of my parachute did not come undone, and I was dragged along by my left leg at ten miles an hour, with my head underneath water. After three minutes I was almost unconscious, when the string came undone. I got my breath back and started swimming.

A rescue craft picked up the unscheduled swimmer ninety minutes later.

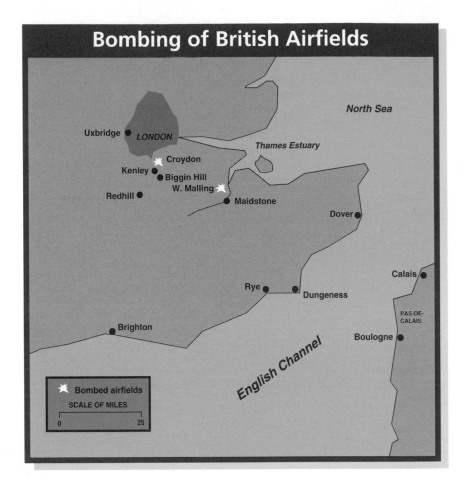

Bombing of British Airfields

North Sea

Uxbridge • | LONDON

Thames Estuary

Croydon

Kenley • • Biggin Hill
W. Malling

Redhill • • Maidstone

Dover •

Calais •

Rye • • Dungeness

PAS-DE-CALAIS

Brighton •

Boulogne •

English Channel

* Bombed airfields
SCALE OF MILES
0   25

squadron in the Group was engaged. There was nothing in re-serve, and the map table showed new waves of attackers crossing the coast." In the air, a young RAF pilot closed with an enemy bomber and sprayed it with an eight-gun burst. The bomber tried to flee. Of his pursuit of the now-smoking enemy bomber, the RAF pilot wrote: "I dived from 30,000 feet to 3,000 feet at such speed that the bottom panel of the aircraft cracked. . . . I had to get that bomber." When the RAF pilot again drew close to the bomber, he saw little flames flickering around its fuselage and wings. The German pilot yanked the bomber into a steep climbing turn. The RAF pilot stayed with him.

"When he got to the top of his climb I was almost on him. I took sight very carefully and gave the button a quick squeeze." The bomber burst into flames and nosed down. The young RAF pilot watched it explode into the ground, setting a small woods afire.

In the chaos of aerial conflict, and further confused by the checkerboard land patterns below, the Luftwaffe bombers couldn't find Biggin Hill, Redhill, and Kenley. One group flew north to Maidstone and mistakenly bombed the airfield at West Malling. A second group, comprising fifteen Me 110s and eight Me 109s from Rubensdörffer's 210 Group, committed a far more serious error.

So far, the Luftwaffe had carefully spared the city of London from bombing attacks. Hitler had declared England's capital city off-limits to bombing for fear that the RAF would respond by bombing Berlin. Luftwaffe operations maps clearly showed all of London as a restricted zone. Nonetheless, Rubensdörffer's 210 Group, set upon by Hurricanes from 111 Squadron, struck down hard on Croydon, a borough of Greater London, which they had mistaken for Kenley. Their bombs ripped open several hangars and destroyed about forty training aircraft on the ground. Worse, however, German bombs strayed into a residential fringe area and destroyed or damaged about two hundred homes. Sixty-two people were killed. Rubensdörffer's mistake would dramatically affect the outcome of Britain's battle for survival.

Hurricanes from 111 Squadron dived to attack 210 Group again as the Germans climbed out of Croydon. The 110s and 109s drew into a defensive circle and worked their way toward the Channel until more Hurricanes from 32 Squadron joined the fight. Rubensdörffer then tried to break for Calais.

Group 210's combat report indicated: "The four other aircraft of the staff flight followed him [Rubensdörffer] in a shallow dive for home. They disappeared into the mist and were not seen again." Rubensdörffer likely met death in a final encounter with Spitfires from 66 Squadron. In addition to their commander, Group 210 lost five more Me 110s and a single Me 109.

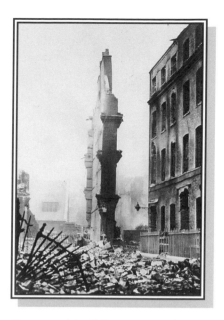

Damaged buildings in London. German bombers mistakenly bombed Croyden, a suburb of London.

"Never in the Field of Human Conflict . . ."

A few scattered night attacks by Luftwaffe bombers that caused only minor damage concluded the third of "three days of the eagle." The Luftwaffe for the first time had used all three of its Air Fleets at the same time, mounting a total of 1,786 sorties to the RAF's 974. German losses for that day tallied seventy-six aircraft against thirty-four for the British. Air Fleet 5 suffered heavily and would never be used again in daylight battle. The vaunted Ju 87 Stuka failed badly as dive-bomber, while the twin-engined Me 110 proved to be a piece of cake for Spitfires and Hurricanes.

At Karinhall, Hermann Göring told his commanders:

It appears necessary to allocate three fighter [groups] to each Stuka [group]. One of these fighter [groups] remains with the Stukas and dives with them to attack; the second flies ahead of the target at medium altitude and engages fighter defenses; the third protects the whole attack from above.

Göring ordered similar protection for his Me 110 destroyer squadrons. These decisions represented huge mistakes in that they prevented the Me 109 fighters from ranging freely to engage and destroy British fighters. By denying his fighters this flexibility, Göring's order effectively removed one of his best chances to eliminate Dowding's Fighter Command.

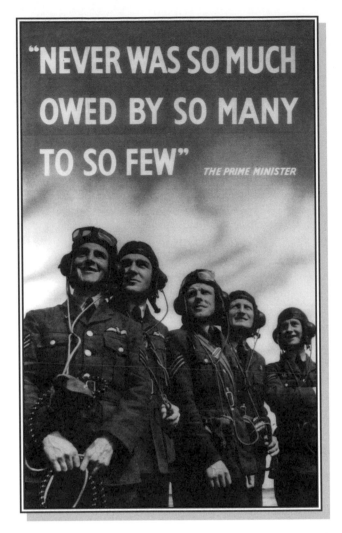

A poster emblazons Prime Minister Churchill's immortal words that have characterized the efforts of the RAF ever since.

"NEVER WAS SO MUCH OWED BY SO MANY TO SO FEW" *THE PRIME MINISTER*

Göring continued his contradictions in command with his next order. Rather than lure British fighters into the air for German fighters to shoot down, he meant now to destroy the RAF on the ground by attacking airfields and aircraft factories.

"Until further orders," Göring declared, "operations are to be directed exclusively against the enemy air force [rather than against Channel shipping, radar stations, and so on], including the targets of the enemy aircraft industry. We must concentrate our efforts on the destruction of the enemy air forces."

Acting on those orders, the Luftwaffe initiated the second phase in the Battle of Britain.

At sundown in Britain on Thursday, August 15, 1940, Winston Churchill and General Ismay left Uxbridge and drove to Chequers, the prime minister's country home. Churchill, rapt in thoughts of the day's events, said to Ismay, "I have never been so moved," then fell silent for about five minutes. Then, leaning forward, Churchill said, "Never in the field of human conflict has so much been owed by so many to so few."

CHAPTER FOUR

Second Phase: The Focus Shifts

"Never climb, never dive; just turn!" The words echoed in British squadron commander Peter Townsend's ears like a song: a song of *survival!* The words formed his maxim for dealing with Messerschmitts. His outmatched Hurricane could yet prevail if only he followed the lyric. He yanked his machine into a tight turn. The 109 on his tail flitted by harmlessly and disappeared beneath him. An instant later, it reappeared in front of him, turning hard to the left. Apparently the German meant to swing around and hit from behind again. A big mistake!

The one thing that a Hurricane could do better than a 109 was turn. Townsend too turned hard and tight to the left, inside the wider-turning Messerschmitt. The British ace caught the full profile of the German craft in his gun sight and buttoned off a short burst. The Messerschmitt flipped over in the air and exploded in a ball of flame. Minutes later, Townsend nailed a second Messerschmitt trying to out-turn him. The maxim worked. It had to.

Britain's survival hinged on the ability of Townsend and other pilots to use every RAF advantage to the fullest, no matter how small it might be. And RAF advantages on August 18, in even the most generous sense, measured small and numbered few.

Two days earlier, on August 16, the Luftwaffe again struck England hard, mounting another 1,715 sorties. The Germans directed most of their attacks against Fighter Command airfields. Among those hardest hit were sector stations—the nerve centers of Dowding's command—at West Malling, Manley, and Tangmere.

A sector represented a geographical subdivision within an air group's (such as Park's No. 11 Group) area of responsibility.

(Above) Fighter ace Peter Townsend (with vest) shot down the first German aircraft that fell on England—long before the Battle of Britain. He continued to effectively score victories over the German fighters and Stukas (right) to help win the Battle of Britain.

Several airfields operated out of a given sector. One station, fully equipped with command, control, and communications apparatus, directed all air operations within each sector. These stations were called sector stations.

No fewer than a dozen Fighter Command squadrons sprang aloft from those bomb-scarred stations to beat back waves of German bombers. But many of the bombers got through. Tangmere and West Malling took hits that put them temporarily out of action.

A Yank in the RAF

At Tangmere, with the enemy attack still under way, American volunteer pilot "Billy" Fiske limped home from a dogfight in his crippled Spitfire. A smoking engine forced him to attempt a landing with his wheels jammed up. Fiske pancaked down on the airstrip and skidded forward through a maze of bomb craters. His Spitfire drew almost to a stop before bursting into flames and exploding. Fiske was fatally wounded. To honor him, grateful Britons later placed an inscribed tablet in St. Paul's Cathedral in memory of "An American citizen who died that England might live."

The Victoria Cross

West of Tangmere, another large force of Ju 87s and Ju 88s under heavy fighter escort attacked airfields at Lee-on-Solent and Gosport. A few raiding bombers dumped bombs on London fringe areas. British and German fighters clashed all along Britain's southern coast. And a later evening attack heavily damaged the airfield at Brize Norton, burning out hangars housing forty-six training aircraft and destroying many other buildings.

In a one-for-one exchange near Southampton that afternoon, a British pilot lost his Hurricane but insisted on payment in kind. Surprised in a sudden attack by an Me 110, RAF flight lieutenant James Nicholson came under heavy machine-gun and cannon fire. One round struck his spare fuel tank, immediately setting his aircraft afire. Additional rounds and metal splinters struck him in the heel, head, and eye. Nearly blinded by blood, he struggled to bail out of his blazing cockpit. Then the German on his tail shot on past Nicholson's doomed Hurricane. Nicholson dropped back into his seat and attacked. With flames blistering his flesh and blood clouding his vision, he managed to get off one long burst. The Me 110 flipped up and over, then plunged into the sea. Only then did Nicholson bail out. He fell several thousand feet before managing with burnt hands to yank his rip cord hard enough to open his parachute. His bulldoglike courage and determination earned him the Victoria Cross, England's highest honor. It was the only "VC" awarded to a fighter pilot in World War II.

The Luftwaffe achieved considerable success on the day but paid for their gains with the loss of forty-nine aircraft, while Fighter Command lost twenty-two valuable fighters.

British Fighter Command Group Areas

North Atlantic Ocean

NO. 13 GROUP

Richard Ernest Saul

NORTHERN IRELAND

North Sea

Irish Sea

NO. 12 GROUP

Trafford Leigh-Mallory

NO. 10 GROUP

NO. 11 GROUP

Keith Park

Sir Christopher Brand

UNITED KINGDOM

Scale of Miles

0   100 Miles

English Channel

A Little Something More

The Luftwaffe onslaught continued. Flying multiple sorties in a day became routine to RAF fighter pilots, as their numbers dwindled in the face of Göring's stepped-up mass attacks. Dedication and courage became their first and last names. Beyond question, their Luftwaffe counterparts displayed similar traits, but the RAF pilots brought a little something more to the battle: the added incentive of fighting for their homeland's survival.

Edward R. Murrow, the noted American war correspondent, captured that spirit in part on a visit to a Fighter Command base:

> As we sat there, they were waiting to take off again. They talked of their own work; discussed the German air force with all the casualness of Sunday-morning halfbacks discussing yesterday's football. There were no nerves, no profanity, and no heroics. There was no swagger about those boys in wrinkled and stained uniforms. When the squadron took off, one of them remarked quite casually that he'd be back in time for tea.

Despite Murrow's description of the seeming casualness of those RAF pilots, extended periods of stress weighed heavily on pilots on both sides.

Luftwaffe ace Adolf Galland later reflected on the burden of such strain: "We saw one comrade after the other, old and tested brothers in combat, vanish from our ranks. Not a day passed

(Below) American war correspondent Edward R. Murrow wrote admiringly of the members of the RAF (right) who fought bravely to victory in spite of being greatly outnumbered by the Germans. Everyone, including the Germans, acknowledged the bravery and dedication of these men.

without a place remaining empty at the mess table. New faces appeared, became familiar, until one day these too would disappear." Simple words best define deep feelings.

On August 17, the Luftwaffe fleets, limited their activity to a few reconnaissance flights. They returned in force on August 18.

RAF Fighter Stations Hit Hard

The Germans struck in massed formations at RAF airfields in Kenley, Croydon, and Biggin Hill. At Kenley, Dornier Do 17s thundered in at levels less than fifty feet, while their Me 109 escorts stayed high to engage the usual stir of Hurricanes and Spitfires. Slicing through a barrage from antiaircraft guns of all calibers, the Dorniers pounded the field with over a hundred bombs. In their destructive wake, they left behind ten wrecked hangars and a trashed operations room.

German Dornier 17s fly above the Thames River in England.

Nine Do 17s of Bomber Unit 76 fared less well at Biggin Hill. Only two 17s escaped the savage antiaircraft fire to make it home safely. Of those two, one was flown by its flight engineer, with a dead pilot beside him.

Such heavy losses would later convince Göring to stop all low-level attacks because of their high cost. Although low-level bombing achieved greater accuracy than conventional high-altitude bombing, Göring felt unwilling to pay the added price. This decision played right into the hands of Dowding and Park. Both men in fact dreaded low-level attacks, which rarely gave sufficient warning and restricted fighter operating space. Göring had erred again.

Heavy action continued into the afternoon, with dive-bombing attacks on Gosport, Thorney Island in Hampshire, and Ford in Sussex. Later, Me 109s strafed the airfield at Manston with cannon and machine-gun fire. Night raids followed, as Luftwaffe bombers again spread out over scattered targets.

The weary pilots of Fighter Command finally closed shop on August 18 after flying 766 sorties and shooting seventy-one German aircraft out of Britain's skies. They winced at their loss of twenty-seven fighters.

A Welcome Break

August 19 brought an unexpected five-day lull in Luftwaffe activities over England. This break in the action, however short, could not have come at a better time for Sir Hugh Dowding. Over the

After a Fight

The strain of always being airborne and at risk, or waiting to become so, took something out of a pilot, as an American RAF aviator, Pilot Officer Art Donahue, later recalled:

I felt strangely tired and lazy, not realizing that this was my initiation to a strange feeling of exhaustion with which I was to get better acquainted in the following days. I didn't want to sleep, but I didn't want to move, or talk, or fly, or anything else either, just relax. It's a feeling that's always pervaded me after a fight or a nerve-racking patrol. As nearly as I can describe it, it is a sensation of being drained completely in every part of your body, though I don't know what of. But you seem to want to surrender to relaxation, sitting or lying inert and absorbing whatever it is back into your system. I've heard many other pilots say they get the same feeling.

And there was the more chilling aspect of fear that overruled every other emotion during every waking moment of the fighter pilot's existence. "The fear made sociable chaps become morose—introverts went on the grog," reflected Wing Commander Innes Westmacott years later. Flight Lieutenant Al Deere agreed.

"I've never believed in the theory that some people don't know fear," Deere said. "I just don't believe that. You sure got frightened every time you went off. You felt quite sick and some chaps used to be sick, like that, physically sick."

past ten days, his Fighter Command had lost 213 Spitfires and Hurricanes. Despite the enormous efforts of Lord Beaverbrook and his aircraft production workers, Britain's output of new fighters had started slipping behind RAF losses. The remarkable Beaverbrook used the lull to great advantage. Aided by the Civilian Repair Organization working twelve-hour shifts to put damaged aircraft back on line, fighter production crews managed to catch up with losses. Dowding then turned to deal with another problem that appeared to be growing more serious by the day.

Dowding's Dilemma

Air Chief Marshal Sir Hugh Dowding's complicated strategy for the defense of Britain, developed over the span of his entire RAF career, depended on absolute cooperation among his fighter groups. Keith Park's No. 11 Group had performed brilliantly in defending Britain's vital southeast sector. On occasion, however, Park needed help from neighboring groups. Dowding could rely on Sir Christopher Brand's No. 10 Group in the southwest sector to back up No. 11 group at a moment's notice. Cooperation from Trafford Leigh-Mallory's No. 12 group to the north of No. 11 Group represented quite another matter.

The service rivalry between Leigh-Mallory and Park appeared to Park to be affecting operations. Leigh-Mallory simply couldn't stand taking orders of any kind from Park. Park eventually complained to Dowding of Leigh-Mallory's failures to provide No. 11 Group with proper assistance when needed. Dowding declined to step in, thinking it better to allow his junior officers to work out their problems between themselves.

Leigh-Mallory's disagreement with Dowding's fighter tactics posed an even greater problem in the face of increasingly massive enemy formations. During the early phase of Dowding's air defense, Leigh-Mallory had urged that Luftwaffe assaults be met "with superior forces and large formations." Dowding had refused to adopt the so-called Big Wing strategy proposed by Leigh-Mallory, preferring to use his fighters in smaller, more flexible units. Both Dowding and Park thought that it would take too long to assemble large formations. Park's No. 11 Group, which received only a few minutes' warning of enemy attacks, could ill afford long delays. But Douglas Bader, the RAF's highly regarded legless fighter ace, supported the views of Leigh-Mallory, his superior.

Bader, squadron leader of Hurricane Squadron 242, believed that Big Wings were worth the extra time for assembling—even to the extent of allowing enemy bombers to hit their targets. The greater force of Big Wings, he felt, would enable RAF fighters to intercept bombers on their way home and destroy them in greater numbers. Also, Bader thirsted for more flying than No. 12 Group had seen so far. Big Wings offered a bigger piece of the action.

Fighter ace Douglas Bader supported Leigh-Mallory's contention that fighter formations should be large— what Leigh-Mallory termed "Big Wing" formations. Others disagreed, arguing that smaller formations were needed to maximize time and flexibility.

Bader pursued the issue further and helped to sway Air Vice Marshal Sholto Douglas, deputy chief of the Air Staff, in favor of Leigh-Mallory's opinions. Dowding, supported by the loyal Park, would have none of it, and he continued to operate under his own policies—without interference from above. Changes enacted by the Air Ministry would not become effective until November 1940.

Friction persisted, though, between Leigh-Mallory and Park, prompting Park to later write:

> Number 12 group was frequently called upon to cover my fighter aerodromes around London which were quite defenseless when I had sent all of my squadrons to intercept near the coast. Number 12 Group, however, always delayed dispatching its reinforcements in order to assemble wings of four to six squadrons which went off in roving sweeps from the South East of England, and on several occasions allowed my fighter aerodromes to be heavily bombed.

Time failed to heal old wounds.

Even as the rivalry between his group leaders persisted, so too did Dowding's determination to defend Britain his way. To risk all by slugging it out with an enemy far superior in numbers seemed unwise to the coldly efficient Dowding. He deeply believed that only his "fighter boys" could prevent a German invasion. He therefore couldn't risk their mass destruction.

"I had information that was not generally known," Sir Hugh wrote later, "about the build-up of invasion forces across the Channel on the one hand, and on the other our own wretched chance of resisting if an attack was made." In short, the RAF must hold.

But now, with the Luftwaffe stepping up attacks on Fighter Command airfields, Sir Hugh found himself caught between a

Terror Attacks Begin

Squadron 609 was patrolling over Portsmouth on August 24 when, according to Pilot Officer David Crook, "Very soon a terrific AA barrage sprang up ahead of us, looking exactly like a large number of dirty cotton-wool puffs in the sky. It was a most impressive barrage; besides all the guns at Portsmouth, all the warships in the harbor and dockyard were firing hard. A moment later, through the barrage and well above us, we saw a large German formation wheeling above Portsmouth. We were too low to be able to do anything about it." Departing from earlier bombing strategies, the Luftwaffe included civilian as well as military targets in their attack plan.

Crook watched the beginning of Göring's "terror" bombing from his Hurricane, later to recall: "I cannot imagine a more flagrant case of indiscriminate bombing. The whole salvo fell right in the middle of Portsmouth, and I could see great spurts of flame and smoke springing up all over the place."

The Germans had struck at Ramsgate in the same way earlier that day, as witnessed by reporter Pratt Boorman. "It was a murderous attack," he wrote. "Most of the damage was to workers' houses in a residential area. A large number suffered."

A Fighter Command intelligence summary released at day's end declared that the raids on Portsmouth and Ramsgate appeared "to be the first instances of deliberate day bombing of town and city property." Many more instances would follow.

---

brick and a boulder. He must defend his airfields at all costs. At the same time, he could not tolerate losses that might threaten his control of the air. It was a dilemma that was about to worsen.

Up from the Ashes

The Luftwaffe resumed operations against Britain on August 24. Changes in Luftwaffe tactics as a result of new orders from Göring became immediately apparent. Bomber groups arrived with fewer bombers but many more escorting fighters. With greater protection, more German bombers made it through defending fighters to score more effectively on Dowding's airfields.

Between August 24 and September 6, the Luftwaffe launched thirty-five massive attacks on Fighter Command bases and aircraft factories. During the same period, Luftwaffe losses numbered 380 planes, but Fighter Command also took a hard hit, losing 286 aircraft.

On the night of August 23–24, in a twenty-four-hour pounding of British targets by about one hundred German bombers, several bombers lost their way and jettisoned their bombs over London. Earlier bombings of London suburbs had been accepted by the British as unintentional. But this time, convinced that there had been a "terror" bombing of their capital, the British struck back in kind.

Eighty-one bombers of the RAF's Bomber Command struck Berlin on the following night. Although the German capital absorbed little damage from the three-hour raid, the bombing exerted a great psychological impact on Berliners, who had been assured for months that British bombers could not get past Luftwaffe defenses. Noted author and journalist William L. Shirer, who was in Berlin at the time, wrote:

> I think the populace of Berlin is more affected by the fact that British planes have been able to penetrate to the center of Berlin without trouble than they are about the first casualties. If the British keep this up, it will have a tremendous effect upon the morale of the people here.

Stukas bomb London. On the night of August 23–24, an air raid over London convinced the British to pay back in kind—by attacking the German capital of Berlin.

"In the Mood to Hit Back"

Winston Churchill wrote after the war:

For fifty-seven nights the bombing of London was unceasing. This constituted an ordeal for the world's largest city, the results of which no one could measure beforehand. Never before was so wide an expanse of houses subjected to such bombardment or so many families required to face its problems and its terrors.

The sporadic raiding of London towards the end of August was promptly answered by us in a retaliatory attack on Berlin. Because of the distance we had to travel, this could only be on a very small scale compared with attacks on London from nearby French and Belgian airfields. The War Cabinet was much in the mood to hit back, to raise the stakes, and to defy the enemy. I was sure they were right, and believed that nothing impressed or disturbed Hitler so much as his realization of British wrath and will-power. In his heart he was one of our admirers. He took, of course, full advantage of our reprisal on Berlin, and publicly announced the previously settled policy of reducing London and other British cities to chaos and ruin. "If they attack our cities," he declared on September 4, "we will simply rub out theirs." He tried his best.

The bombing of Germany did not end after the first revenge attacks by the RAF, but continued throughout the course of the war.

The British did keep it up. RAF bombers struck at Berlin a second time, killing many Berliners. Then Dusseldorf, Essen, and several other German cities became RAF targets during a week of "payback" raids. Hitler and Göring were incensed.

Göring's new policy of hitting Dowding's fighters where they lived had battered Fighter Command into near extinction. But just when a German victory was as close as it ever got, an irate Adolf Hitler ordered Göring to lift the devastating Luftwaffe attack on RAF fighter bases, control centers, and aircraft factories.

The battle focus shifted once again, this time to the unrelenting bombing of London. And up from the ash, flame, and rubble of London Town, the badly ruffled birds of Fighter Command slicked back their feathers and rose to fight on.

CHAPTER FIVE

September 15: Battle of Britain Day

At Berlin's *Sportpalast* (sports arena) on September 4, 1940, in an address to the German people, Adolf Hitler said: "In England they're filled with curiosity and keep asking, 'Why doesn't he come?' Be calm. Be calm. He's coming! He's coming!" He made known his intentions to the British three days later.

By order of a directive from German Supreme Headquarters, the first intentional bombing of London commenced on September 7. For once, the Luftwaffe caught Fighter Command by surprise.

Among the few RAF pilots to rise against the German swarm was Pilot Officer George Barclay of Hurricane Squadron 249. An

(Above) Suited men watch for German bombers atop the U.S. embassy. (Left) London during the first mass air raid. The raid commenced in the late afternoon, and after a short pause was renewed and continued throughout the night.

awesome sight greeted him: "There, several miles away, was a black line in the sky," he recalled later. "Thirty-five Hun bombers in close formation—I gradually began to distinguish about 70 to 100 other little dots—fighters." Barclay and his squadron mates turned to attack the bombers:

> But before one could take stock of the situation the Messerschmitts were on me. I turned quickly to see if there was anything on my tail and at that same moment two 109s went past beneath my nose. I turned, diving on one and gave him a burst—nothing happened. Presumedly I had missed him, but the noise of my eight guns gave me great confidence. I gave a second Me 109 a burst. A sudden flash of brilliant flame, a cloud of smoke, and a vast piece flew off, and down he went.

"London Is in Flames"

More than three hundred tons of bombs rained down on London that day in under an hour and a half. The East End and dock areas absorbed most of the punishment. The Luftwaffe's brute force overwhelmed Fighter Command, downing thirty-eight RAF planes and killing or wounding twenty RAF pilots. Four hundred and forty-eight Londoners died and more than a thousand suffered injuries, as the savage bombing continued through the night. The Germans lost twenty-nine aircraft.

That evening, a joyful Göring broadcast a radio message of pure delight: "This is the historic hour when for the first time our Air Force delivered its thrust right into the enemy's heart! . . . London is in flames."

Down but Not Out

Despite his dismay over London's ordeal, Sir Hugh Dowding's first concern rested with his fighters, Britain's last hope. The air chief marshal recognized at once that Hitler had spitefully yielded to the temptation of bombing London, rather than continuing attacks on more critical airfield and aircraft factory targets.

Earlier, while developing his strategy for the defense of Britain, Dowding had predicted that "the nearness of London to German airfields will lose them the war." His crystal ball appeared to be working. The shift in German strategy away from attacks on RAF airfields would shortly allow Fighter Command sufficient time to recover from a near-knockout blow. They would return.

Working from emergency fireboats, firemen send streams of water into a burning building, fired by the German air raids on the Dockland area of London.

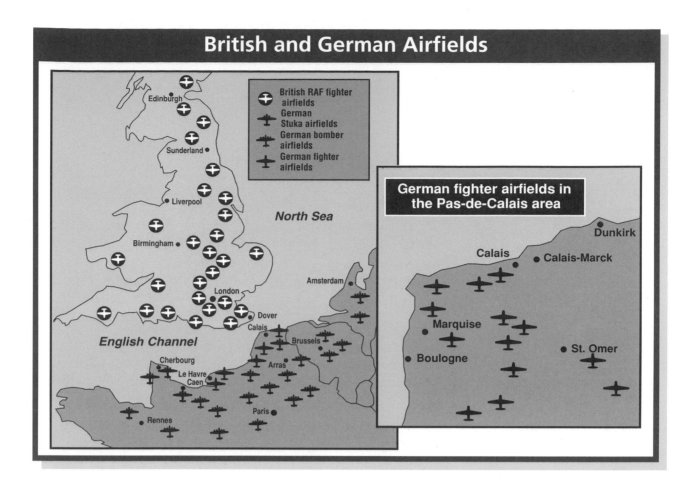

British and German Airfields

Legend:
- British RAF fighter airfields
- German Stuka airfields
- German bomber airfields
- German fighter airfields

North Sea

Edinburgh
Sunderland •
• Liverpool
Birmingham •
London
Dover
Calais
Amsterdam •
Brussels
English Channel
Cherbourg
Le Havre
Caen
Arras
Rennes •
Paris •

German fighter airfields in the Pas-de-Calais area

Dunkirk
Calais • Calais-Marck
Marquise
Boulogne •
St. Omer •

The importance of Hitler's decision to divert the Luftwaffe from its assault on Fighter Command to the vengeance-inspired bombing of London can never be overstated. That decision quite possibly cost Germany victory in World War II. It allowed Dowding to concentrate the fighters over London, rather than having to defend the entire island with his rapidly diminishing forces. It further provided the British with sufficient time to train pilots to replace those who had been killed or injured and to manufacture and repair additional aircraft. Although responsibility for the fateful decision rests solidly with Hitler, it should be remembered that the decision had the full and enthusiastic support of Hermann Göring.

The bombing of London continued through a second night of horror, killing another 412 Londoners. But Dowding regrouped his defenses quickly. The next day, September 9, Keith Park's No. 11 Group, with some help from No. 12 Group, greeted more than two hundred German bombers when Kesselring's Air Fleet 2 reappeared over England. During a textbook display of tactics, the RAF destroyed twenty-eight German aircraft against a loss of nineteen fighters.

Fighter Command's stiff resistance gave Göring pause. But he continued to believe that the Luftwaffe would finally destroy the

RAF in another few days of fighting. Hitler apparently didn't share Göring's confidence. On September 10, the Führer postponed until September 14 (and later until September 17) any final decision to proceed with Operation Sea Lion.

Poor weather conditions then temporarily interfered with daytime bombing operations, but the night raids continued, night after night. Luftwaffe bombs killed some two thousand more Londoners and injured an additional ten thousand between September 8 and September 14. Göring, now convinced that only a handful of British fighters remained operational, prepared to strike a final blow for air supremacy on September 15. History will record the date for now and ever as *the* day of days when once again "the few" fought the Battle of Britain.

Making History

Sunday, September 15, 1940, in the words of Air Vice Marshal Keith Park, was "one of those days of autumn when the countryside was at its loveliest." At 1045 Park greeted Winston Churchill and his wife, Clementine, in No. 11 Group's underground operations room at Uxbridge. "I don't know whether anything will happen today," Park said to them. "At present all is quiet."

Scenes of London during the massive German air raids. (Below) A "tube" station is converted into a shelter for those made homeless by the bombs. (Right) The devastation of the air raids is clearly seen in this photo taken from St. Paul's Cathedral.

Observer Corps

In addition to directing Fighter Command from his headquarters at Bentley Priory, Air Chief Marshal Sir Hugh Dowding claimed responsibility for the operational control of the Observer Corps, the Balloon Command, and the Anti-Aircraft Command. The Balloon Command flew large barrage balloons over vulnerable targets from small, mobile winch lorries, forcing enemy aircraft to fly at greater heights. Most German planes flew above the range of the Anti-Aircraft Command's outdated guns, thus the gunners rarely scored direct hits. Their importance to civilian morale cannot be undervalued, however, in the sense that Britons were striking back at the hated Luftwaffe. Of greater defensive importance was the role of the Observer Corps.

An organization of trained volunteer aircraft spotters, the Observer Corps was an outgrowth of Major General E.B. Ashmore's World War I control and reporting network, originally established to counter the threat of German Gotha and Staaken bombers. By 1940 the Observer Corps had grown to more than thirty group reporting centers, each center connected to several of the thousand observer posts. A post comprised some twenty operatives who alternated duties of observing, reporting, and calculating identified units.

Spotters determined aircraft types through the use of charts or by memory. By means of a device called the Mickelthwait Height Correction Attachment, which was fitted to a circular plotting base, observers could determine aircraft height and direction information. Observer posts would pass along information to group reporting centers, which in turn would relay the information to affected sector stations. Finally, the data would be forwarded to Fighter Command headquarters at Bentley Priory.

At 1100, plotters of the Women's Auxiliary Air Force started moving magnetic markers across the huge map of Britain and the Channel. The markers represented a massive force of one hundred Dornier bombers and four hundred fighters then approaching the coast of England. The huge Luftwaffe formation crossed the coast at 1130. Eleven of Park's squadrons awaited the advancing Germans.

In addition to the RAF's vital radar network and early warning system, information provided by British Intelligence helped Sir Hugh Dowding's pilots to "prepare the table" for German visitors. Dowding knew in advance how many Germans were coming, when and where they would strike, and that the attack would come in two waves. Park sent every available fighter pilot aloft, with instructions to return directly after engaging the enemy, refuel quickly, and hustle back upstairs to welcome the second wave.

From No. 10 Group to his west, Park requested and used help from one squadron to cover his flank. In Leigh-Mallory's sector to the north, Squadron Leader Douglas Bader sprang into the air and assembled five squadrons of what by then was called the Duxford wing of No. 12 Group. Bader's assignment was to cover Park's unprotected airfields along the northern perimeter of London, but he led his Big Wing farther south. Bader was not about to miss what he later described as "the finest shambles I've ever been in."

Spitfires of the 72 and 92 Squadrons clashed first with Dorniers of Bomber Unit 3 over Canterbury. The Spitfires, once defined by British ace Stanford Tuck as "thirty feet of wicked beauty," slashed through the bomber formation, sending several Dorniers down in smoking defeat. The "beauties" had drawn first blood.

Messerschmitt Me 109s joined the battle as it drifted across Kent toward London. The Germans, thinking that Fighter Command had been all but eliminated, became rattled when met by such strong RAF resistance. The Dorniers that managed to reach London missed most of their targets. But one Luftwaffe bomb struck Buckingham Palace, the principal residence of King George VI of England and his family.

Hurricane pilot Sergeant Ray Holmes of 504 Squadron spotted the offending Dornier and two others. He decided "to give them a little attention." With only fifteen seconds of firing time left, he whipped his Hurricane around for a frontal attack. "I thought a head-on attack might cool his ardor," he said later. Holmes bore in and emptied his guns in the face of the onrushing Dornier.

Passing over the top of the bomber, Holmes remembered that he "clipped one side of his fragile-looking twin tail with my port wing." He felt a slight bump. The Hurricane's wing dropped, then the nose, and then the controls quit responding. The tip of his wing had been torn off. His machine snapped over into a vertical roll, forcing Holmes to bail out. But the Dornier went down too.

The king and queen inspect the damage to Buckingham Palace after Nazi raiders attacked.

Squadron Leader Bryan Lane of No. 19 Squadron entered the action over the Thames and later made this entry in his logbook: "Ran into the whole Luftwaffe. Wave after wave of bombers covered by several hundred fighters. Waded into escort as per arrangement and picked out a 109. Had a hell of a dogfight."

A German Viewpoint

German ace Adolf Galland, who led his Fighter Unit 26 in a forward free hunt, recalls attacking and downing a Hurricane after ten minutes of furious fighting:

German air ace Adolf Galland took part in the raids on London.

> I had damaged her badly and she was on fire. She ought to have been a dead loss. Yet she did not crash but glided down in gentle curves. My flight companions and I attacked her three times—without a final result. I flew close alongside the flying wreck, by now thoroughly riddled, with smoke belching from her. From a distance of a few yards I saw the dead pilot sitting in his shattered cockpit, while his aircraft spiralled slowly to the ground as though piloted by a ghostly hand.

> I can only express the highest admiration for the British fighter pilots, who, although technically at a disadvantage, fought bravely and [tirelessly]. They undoubtedly saved their country in this crucial hour.

The long distances to home base limited German fighters to runs of short duration over Britain. This constituted a major RAF advantage. With the red fuel light blinking in his cockpit, Galland broke for home rather than end up out of fuel in the Channel. He had passed that way before, as he later explained:

> The short range of the Me 109 became more and more of a problem. During a single sortie of my wing we lost 12 fighter planes, not by enemy action, but simply because after two hours' flying time the bombers we were escorting had not yet reached the mainland on their return journey. Five of these fighters managed to make a pancake landing on the French shore with their last drop of fuel, seven of them landed in the "drink."

Such visions no doubt came to mind as Galland winged his way homeward.

Bader's Big Wing

Visions of a different sort—visions of British fighters everywhere—became a reality right then for German bomber crews over London. Bader's Big Wing, appearing on scene from the north, represented an awesome sight to the Germans, who had been informed by Luftwaffe intelligence chief Josef "Beppo" Schmid that Fighter Command's aircraft had dwindled to its last fifty. The Big Wing alone comprised *sixty* fighters from Bader's own No. 242 Squadron, the Czech No. 310, and the Polish No. 302, all flying Hurricanes, as well as two Spitfire squadrons, Nos. 19 and 611.

Bader immediately spotted forty or more Junkers Ju 88s and Dornier Do 17s, and off in the distance the telltale flyspecks of a German fighter escort. He warned his squadron mates of the approaching fighters over his radio transmitter. Then, nosing over toward the German bombers, he shouted, "Break 'em up!"

Bader tore into the face of the bomber formation with eight guns chattering. In the middle of the pack, he kicked rudder and whirled his Hurricane around on the tail of a Dornier. He let go a burst, then another. The Dornier's starboard engine flashed light and erupted in flame. Black smoke spewed from it. The Hurricane almost smashed into the Dornier, but Bader broke off just in time. Then he found himself in the midst of a jumble of swooping, turning, climbing, whirling machines, caught in a deadly struggle to destroy or be destroyed.

Four hundred yards to his front, Bader glimpsed another Dornier seeking to hide in a layered cloud formation. In a flash of action, he sighted a diving Spitfire from the corner of his eye. The Spitfire pilot never saw the Dornier and smacked headlong into the middle of the bomber's slender frame. The Dornier exploded in flames. Its wings collapsed and cradled the Spitfire. They plunged to earth together locked in a flaming embrace.

Bader, twisting about in a sweat, scanned the neighborhood for another likely target and caught sight of yet another Dornier to one side and below. He watched it plunging earthward, flaming and

Bader's "Big Wing" squadron, credited with over sixty-eight victories during the Battle of Britain, surprised the German fighters over London.

trailing smoke. Suddenly a crew member leaped from the fiery hulk. His parachute opened but far too soon. Its silken canopy caught fire and collapsed. Shroud lines strung out behind the unlucky German and grasped at air. He dropped like an iron eagle.

Seemingly without pity, Bader muttered to himself, "Good show, you rat. Now you've got a little time to think about it and there isn't any answer." Bader turned to search the skies again and found them empty. Back at Duxford at day's end, Bader's 242 Squadron claimed twelve victories.

Leigh-Mallory telephoned Bader that evening and said, "What a wonderful show today! It's absolutely clear your big formations are paying big dividends." But were they?

Bader answered, "Thank you very much, sir, but we had a sticky time on the second trip. They scrambled us too late again and the Germans were a long way above us when we spotted them."

Bader's response to Leigh-Mallory's congratulations singled out one of the main reasons Dowding and Park refused to adopt Big Wing practices: The massive formations *simply could not react fast enough.*

At the height of the battle, Winston Churchill watched the red "At Readiness" lights go out, one by one, on the display board back in Park's Uxbridge operations room. A red light indicated a squadron that was standing by and ready for action. When the last light went out, Churchill asked, "What other reserves have we?"

Park replied, "None."

Although Park meant reserves immediately available from his own No. 11 Group, exclusive of possible help from Nos. 10 and 12 Groups, his situation was grim and growing grimmer. His pilots aloft would soon need refueling. If the Luftwaffe mounted another massive assault when No. 11 Group's planes came down for refueling and servicing, Park's aircraft would be caught out of action. He would be unable to defend his sector at the most critical point in the entire Battle of Britain. But that didn't happen.

The "Greatest Day"

A brief calm settled over the English countryside at about 1230. The fighting resumed shortly before 1430, however, when the Luftwaffe struck again, harder. Three massed formations crossed the British shoreline between Dungeness and Dover. Fighters met them again and fought a running battle toward London. The weight of Luftwaffe numbers alone made it almost impossible for Fighter Command to turn back the Germans before they reached the city. Moreover, German bombers seemed to be getting harder to kill—at least according to RAF pilot John Sample of 504 Squadron, who wrote:

> I attacked him [German bomber] four times altogether. I fired at him from the left, swung over the right, turned in towards

Maintenance Magic

"Quick refueling and rearming practices gave ground crews the sleight of hand which speeded their tasks and gained precious seconds," Squadron Leader Peter Townsend wrote later. "Between them and the pilots existed an understanding on which our lives depended. The slightest grumble from an engine, or any other functional defect—it might occur five miles above ground or ten miles from the coast—had to be explained to our fitters or riggers, or to the armorers or radio mechanics, in the terms and nuances of their technical language. We would provide the clue but we relied implicitly on their vigilance, skill, and devotion to keep our machines free of defects which could cost us our lives." Ground crews "kept 'em flyin'," as did Lord Beaverbrook's aircraft manufacturing and repair workers.

"The activities of Beaverbrook's Ministry of Aircraft Production went beyond the mere production of aircraft," Townsend noted. "Damaged aircraft had to be made new and a formidable organization existed to this end: the Civilian Repair Organization. In February 1940 it repaired a total of 20 machines; in July it would repair 160. Of all the fighters supplied during the Battle of Britain 35 percent would be repair jobs—as good as new."

another hollow in the cloud, where I expected him to reappear, and fired at him again. After my fourth attack he dived down headlong into a clump of trees in front of a house.

Bader's Big Wing showed up again about 1440 over Dartford, where Bader witnessed another extraordinary parachute descent that he later described:

> One unfortunate German rear-gunner bailed out of the Dornier 17 I attacked, but his parachute caught on the tail. There he was, swinging helplessly, with the aircraft swooping and diving and staggering all over the sky. That bomber went crashing into the Thames Estuary, with the swinging gunner still there.

Far below the conflict, Londoners craned their necks and looked skyward to witness the greatest air battle of that day or any other. Göring's flawed estimates of British fighter strength were written off by Sir Hugh's "fighter boys" for once and for all and for all to see. The truth was etched for time everlasting by the thin, white contrails of Spitfires and Hurricanes, scribing their legend against a background of royal blue. In England, they called it the "greatest day," and indeed it was.

(Below) Londoners crane their necks to watch German and British aces (right) fight it out above their heads.

Aftermath

Scores of German bombers jettisoned their bombs and streaked for home, rather than face the rising fury of Britain's eight-gun defenders. A later tally of the day's action revealed that forty Luftwaffe bombers and sixteen fighters failed to make it home. The RAF lost twenty-six machines and thirteen pilots, with thirteen airmen parachuting to safety. The next day, Winston Churchill broadcast a reassuring message to all Britons. He said, in part:

> Yesterday eclipsed all previous records of Fighter Command. Aided by squadrons of their Czech and Polish comrades, using only a small proportion of their total strength and under cloud conditions of some difficulty, they cut to rags and tatters three separate waves of murderous assault upon the civil population of their native land, inflicting a certain loss of one hundred and twenty-five bombers and fifty-three fighters upon the enemy to say nothing of the probables and damages, while themselves sustaining a loss of twelve pilots and twenty-five machines. These results exceed all expectations and give just and sober confidence in the approaching struggle.

The prime minister exaggerated when he said "using only a small proportion of their total strength" so as not to reveal the true strength of Fighter Command. He also inflated Luftwaffe losses in his speech and shaved British losses. Also, he included a final, early evening raid by 20 Messerschmitt Me 110 light bombers as the third of "three separate waves of murderous assault." The "wave" of 110s, distracted by heavy antiaircraft fire, missed its targets and hardly compared to the morning and afternoon attacks. But at the time, Britons needed a morale builder and Churchill once again delivered one.

Across the Channel, Luftwaffe chief Hermann Göring continued to claim that his service would eliminate the RAF within four or five days. On September 16, other high-ranking German officers took a different view. The RAF obviously remained a strong defensive factor, they argued; and the summer days of calm seas and clear skies, essential to a successful invasion, were rapidly slipping away. The German naval staff in particular wanted no part of Operation Sea Lion and conveyed their misgivings to the Führer.

A brief entry for September 17 in the German Naval War Diary indicated Hitler's response to the doubts expressed by some of his top advisers: "The enemy Air Force is still by no means defeated. On the contrary, it shows increasing activity. The weather situation as a whole does not permit us to expect a period of calm. . . . *The Führer therefore decides to postpone 'Sea Lion' indefinitely."*

The italics are the German navy's.

Hitler was *not* coming, after all—not in the summer of 1940. Hitler was not coming *ever.*

CHAPTER SIX

Third Phase: Winding Down and Summing Up

In an official dispatch issued after the RAF's "greatest day," Fighter Command's Air Chief Marshal Sir Hugh Dowding stated: "Heavy pressure was kept up until September 27, but by the end of the month it became apparent that the Germans could no longer face the bomber wastage which they had sustained." Britain's defenders then felt confident enough that Hitler indeed was not "coming" to relax their highest state of invasion alert on September 17.

On September 18, the Luftwaffe struck at London again with a flight of some seventy bombers. RAF fighters intercepted and turned away the bombers after a savage aerial encounter.

A Third Great Day

In the early morning of September 27, Göring, in what appeared to be a fit of temper, launched another major daylight assault on England. A wave of Messerschmitt Me 110s, carrying bombs and accompanied by a heavy escort of 109s, turned inland over Dungeness. Dowding's fighter boys met the Germans at once and pecked away at them all the way to London. The confused Germans finally broke formation and turned for home, scattering bombs willy-nilly about the countryside.

Even as the Messerschmitts fled, two strong groups of Ju 88s and Do 17s crossed the British coast and droned steadily on toward London. No. 11 Group Hurricanes and Spitfires eight-gunned the Germans into reconsidering their destination, and they too broke and raced back across the Channel.

Later that afternoon, a German bomber force some three hundred strong also set course for London and met with a similar end. Within sight of the capital, RAF fighters chopped up the bombers badly and forced them to turn tail and make tracks for home.

A final pass against Bristol by eighty Luftwaffe bombers brought the Germans their only success of the day, as a few of their bombs struck the city. By nightfall, the RAF had knocked down fifty-five German aircraft. Although losing twenty-eight fighters of their own, British pilots had won another decisive victory.

An impressed Winston Churchill wrote words of praise to the secretary of state for air the next morning: "Pray congratulate the Fighter Command on the results of yesterday. The scale and intensity of the fighting and the heavy losses of the enemy make September 27 rank with September 15 and August 15 as the third great and victorious day of the Fighter Command during the course of the Battle of Britain."

Messerschmitt 110s fly over England.

Winding Down

The last large-scale daylight attack on London occurred on September 30—the Luftwaffe's last surge in the sun. The Germans lost forty-seven more aircraft.

An angry Hermann Göring, shattered by the news of the Luftwaffe's continuing losses, typically blamed the losses on his fighter arm. The fighters, Göring believed, simply were not providing proper protection for his bombers. He chose to ignore the effects on the performance of the Luftwaffe's fighter arm of his own poor decisions. As his problems mounted, Göring demanded to hear from Adolf Galland what it would take to solve them.

The rising fighter ace, destined to become the Fighter-General of the Luftwaffe, replied, "A Gruppe [group] of Spitfires."

Göring could have done worse.

On October 1, Göring initiated yet another change in strategy by launching a string of fighter-bomber raids on Britain. The Luftwaffe chief had ordered 250 fighters—about one-third of his fighter arm—converted to fighter-bombers. If the fighter arm could not protect his bombers, Göring reasoned, then the fighters must take responsibility for delivering the bombs themselves. This tactic supposedly would provide an added bonus by freeing the bombers for night raids, which did not require fighter protection.

Adolf Galland didn't think much of Göring's idea. "The fighter-bombers were put into action in a great hurry," he wrote. "There was hardly time to give the pilots bombing training."

With little heart for Göring's latest whim, German fighter pilots found it convenient to dump their bombs anywhere when attacked by RAF fighters, rather than press on to their assigned targets. Such occurrences would lead in to a period of high-altitude, one-on-one fighter confrontations over Britain later in the year. But Göring's fighter-as-bomber idea soon proved to have, in Galland's words, "no more than nuisance value."

During October, with the days growing shorter and the autumn weather worsening, daylight operations over Britain slowly tapered off to an occasional dogfight. The daytime war was all but over.

"The Blitz"

But the Luftwaffe's nighttime assaults on Britain remained far from over, as Winston Churchill would point out later in his memoirs:

> The first German aim had been the destruction of our air power; the second was to break the spirit of the Londoner, or at least render uninhabitable the world's largest city. In these new purposes the enemy did not succeed. The victory of the Royal Air Force had been gained by the skill and daring of our pilots, by the excellence of our machines, and by their wonderful organization.

> Other virtues not less splendid, not less indispensable to the life of Britain, were now to be displayed by millions of ordinary humble people, who proved to the world the strength of a community nursed in freedom.

Britons displayed those splendid and indispensable virtues during phase three of the Battle of Britain, when, as the prime

British citizens display "what they're made of" amid the ruins of London. Citizens managed to keep their spirits up even though they underwent frightening air raids nightly.

minister wrote, "an average of two hundred German bombers attacked London every night." Fifty-seven times, without missing a night from September 7 through November 2, German bombers kept their fearful appointment over London. Those night attacks on the British capital became known as "the Blitz."

The mournful cries of air raid warning signals—or "Wailing Winnies"—rang out routinely each of those fifty-seven nights. And long fingers of light probed the heavens in search of winged intruders from hell. Britons crouched in sandbagged cellars and concrete subway tunnels and listened to the night music of crump-crumping antiaircraft guns and bombs whining and bursting all around them. The HE (high-explosive) bombs introduced Londoners to a terror almost beyond description.

Len Jones, who was eighteen years old when he experienced the London blitz in King Street, Poplar, recalled one such night of horror: "The suction and the compression from the high explosive blasts just pulled and pushed you . . . you could actually feel your eyeballs being sucked out. I was holding my eyes to try and stop them from going."

Ordinary People

A Practical Guide for the Householder and Air-Raid Warden, published in England in 1940, provided British civilians with a vivid description of the effects of a large, high-explosive (HE) bomb: "Within 50 feet of a large bomb its wind-blast will tear a man to pieces and will shatter a brick wall. Further away, the blast will deafen people by bursting their ear-drums, and may kill them by paralyzing their lungs." The people of Coventry, England, experienced the devastating effects of such bombs as much as or more than any other British householders.

On November 14, 1940, the Luton (England) *News* reported: "Just after tea German bombers flew over Luton for hour after hour on their way to the Midland city of Coventry." That night, in one of the most savage attacks of the war, Luftwaffe bombs killed at least 554 people and seriously injured 865 more.

A report issued the next day by *Mass Observation*, an organization of English pollsters, captured the bleak reality of a city in the aftermath of an HE bomb-storm: "In Coventry . . . there were more open signs of hysteria, terror, neurosis observed than during the whole of the previous two months together in all areas. Women were seen to cry, to scream, to tremble all over, to faint in the street, to attack a fireman, and so on. The overwhelmingly dominant feeling on Friday was the feeling of utter helplessness. The tremendous impact of the previous night had left people practically speechless in many cases. And it made them feel impotent [powerless]. There was no role for the civilian. Ordinary people had no idea what they should do."

In an air raid shelter, this London couple manage to find room for a bed for the wife and a deck chair for the husband.

Moving to a nearby air raid shelter, Jones experienced the same kind of frightening suction: "It [the shelter] was lifting and moving, rolling almost as if it was a ship in a rough sea . . . the suction and the blasts coming in and out of the steel door . . . was smashing backwards and forwards and bashed us all around against the walls."

As fearsome as the HE bombs were, incendiary bombs caused even more destruction. Hundreds of these devices tumbled down upon London, setting the city ablaze from one end to the other. Correspondent Edward R. Murrow, on his regular Sunday night radio broadcast, described for some thirty million American listeners an earlier glimpse of London burning.

"This . . . is London," Murrow opened gravely. He always began his broadcasts from London with these words. Then he continued: "The fire up the river had turned the moon blood-red . . . huge pear-shaped bursts of flame would rise up into the smoke and disappear . . . the world was upside down."

Later, broadcasting from a London rooftop on a late September afternoon, Murrow reported seeing "many flags flying from many staffs. No one told these people to put out the flag. They simply feel like flying the Union Jack [the British colors] above their roof." The display moved Murrow to say, "No flag up there was white."

The bombing of London and other principal British cities continued until May 10, 1941, when Hitler turned the might of the Luftwaffe eastward to attack Russia. In eight months, the blitz killed more than four hundred thousand civilians, injured another forty-six thousand people, and destroyed a million homes. Those on the home front also served.

The Führer had long planned to reclaim lands lost to Russia in World War I. He also felt that England would eventually give in to the Nazi submarine blockade of Britain and seek a negotiated peace. So, over the objections of many of his generals, Hitler opened a second front in the east. Hitler had allowed his abiding hatred of Russians and the communist government then in power in the Soviet Union to overrule his reason. He would soon regret it.

Edward R. Murrow gave a regular Sunday night radio program to update Americans about the Battle of Britain. He always began his broadcasts with the words "This is London."

For Services Rendered

Fighter Command's Air Chief Marshal Sir Hugh Dowding and his strong right arm, No. 11 Group's Air Vice Marshal Keith Park, won the Battle of Britain. The long view of history over five decades of analysis supports that premise beyond question. It would seem therefore to follow that these two courageous men must have shared in the honors a country traditionally bestows on its heroes.

But they did not.

On October 17, 1940, Dowding and Park were called by

Seldom Grateful

"Dowding had all along been the architect of victory," Squadron Leader Peter Townsend wrote, "laboring over four years in the conviction that it could be won only 'by science thoughtfully applied to operational requirements.' His principal commander, Park, was the master tactician; with a greatly outnumbered fighting force he had outwitted and repulsed a courageous, determined enemy.

"But the victorious air marshals, at whose hands Hitler had suffered his first defeat, were not acclaimed," Townsend went on. "Dowding, it is true, was raised, on September 30, to the dignity of Knight Grand Commander of Bath. Soon afterward he was replaced by Sholto Douglas as Commander-in-Chief, Fighter Command. Park was also replaced—by Leigh-Mallory—and relegated [banished], one might say, to Training Command.

"The two victors thus realized the sad truth—that men are seldom grateful for their saviors. But in this case the British people, themselves under heavy fire from the enemy, could be forgiven for not knowing that they owed their salvation to Dowding and Park, especially as both men remained in the background throughout the Battle.

"Shortly before being removed from their posts, both were summoned to appear before the Air Council, not to be thanked, but to answer for their conduct of operations. They had vanquished the foe . . . but not, apparently, in the approved fashion."

Deputy Chief of the Air Staff Sholto Douglas to attend a critical meeting at the Air Ministry. Air Vice Marshal Trafford Leigh-Mallory and Squadron Leader Douglas Bader were also in attendance. The purpose of the meeting was to explore why Dowding and Park in turn had failed to adopt the Big Wing principle. Unfortunately for Dowding and Park, Sholto Douglas already held strong opinions in favor of Big Wings. Park said later that he felt as if he were on trial and that Sholto Douglas was "the public prosecutor." In truth, Park, along with Dowding, stood accused of mishandling their forces. Park spoke in defense of himself and his chief:

> I explained to the august gathering that it was a time and distance problem. The short warning I received of the approach of the enemy formations was not time enough for me to dispatch, assemble, climb and maneuver wings of three, let alone five, squadrons before [the enemy] had unloaded bombs on vital targets.

> I explained that I should [would] have lost the Battle of Britain had I allowed uninterrupted bombing of fighter airdromes, aircraft factories—and London. . . . Further, my clumsy fighter wings would themselves have been attacked by enemy fighters who had the advantage of height and sun.

Leigh-Mallory then spoke briefly, emphasizing that big formations worked handsomely when allowed to assemble first in airfields in the rear. Park hardly agreed with that judgment, in that several of his airfields had been blasted to bits, some under the very noses of Leigh-Mallory's No. 12 Group fighters. Park felt less than comfortable with the idea of keeping his fighters on the ground and relying on No.12 Group to protect them.

"Leigh-Mallory floundered a bit," Park recalled, "then called on Squadron Leader Bader."

Bader stressed the point that "it is much more economical to put up a hundred aircraft against a hundred than twelve against a hundred." It was a valid argument.

Park himself had on occasion put more than 250 fighters in the air at one time—on September 15, for example—but in smaller, more flexible groups of one or two dozen. Bader pressed forward with his own ideas, growing in self-confidence and showing considerable command presence.

"I know we can't always put equal numbers against the Germans," he said, "because their air force is bigger than ours—if necessary we'll fight one against a thousand—but surely we can manage to put sixty aircraft against a couple of hundred instead of only one squadron of twelve."

Since Park had operated with Dowding's complete knowledge and consent, Park felt that the day's meeting had been

Keith Park, commanding officer of No. 11 Group, helped to win the Battle of Britain with the small, flexible units of squadrons advocated by Dowding. He was fired for his efforts.

called solely to condemn Dowding and himself. "The wings controversy," Park said, "was used as a pretext for dismissing Dowding. I was also sacked."

On November 16, as a reward for services rendered, Dowding received a phone call from Britain's secretary of state for air asking him to resign. He was denied even the customary letter confirming his resignation and noting his accomplishments. In place of routine courtesies, Dowding was told that he might make himself useful "investigating service waste." Sholto Douglas replaced Dowding and was promoted to marshal of the Royal Air Force, a rank that had been withheld from Dowding.

Commander in chief of Fighter Command was a post normally occupied for three years. Dowding had filled it for four years. Because of having served an extra year, he never protested his removal.

In an interview with an American reporter twenty-eight years later, Dowding said, "I felt a bit sorry having to retire in the middle of a war. But they had every justification in putting somebody else in instead." Many thought otherwise.

The official history of the Battle of Britain issued in 1941 did not mention Sir Hugh Dowding.

Keith Park was replaced as commander of No. 11 Group by Leigh-Mallory and posted to Training Command. He later spoke in

Galland Assesses the Battle

"The [German] fighter pilots who took part in the Battle of Britain were quite justly convinced that they had done their duty during the past weeks of heavy fighting," Adolf Galland wrote after the war. "They had accepted heavy losses in unflagging action combined with outstanding successes, but never once did they question the final aim or how long this murderous battle was going to last."

Germany's fighter-general continued, "The overall fighting strength of the Luftwaffe was reduced to three quarters compared with the beginning of the Battle of Britain," Adolf Galland wrote after the war. "It is therefore wrong to speak either of annihilation or of a decisive defeat of the German Luftwaffe in this battle. Those who express the point of view that the back of our air force was broken and that it was never again in a position to recover from this blow misunderstood the real situation. This error must be corrected in the interests of history. It is true to say that the cessation of German day raids on London was an outstanding and brilliant English success of both military and political importance. The last phase, too, of the Battle of Britain was to be a great worry to the English population and to their war leaders. But the immediate, the mortal danger was overcome. England had passed victoriously through one of the most serious ordeals in her history. She never lost her courage or her self-confidence. Staggering and bleeding, but with clenched teeth, she stood fast during the critical round."

A British fighter base somewhere in southern England. With tenacity and with luck—Hitler decided to give up on Britain and attack Russia—the RAF won the Battle of Britain.

sharper terms than had Dowding about their rewards for services rendered: "To my dying day I shall feel bitter at the base intrigue [gross finagling] which was used to remove Dowding and myself as soon as we had won the Battle of Britain."

Summing Up

During the 116 days between July 10 and October 31, 1940, a thin blue line of Royal Air Force defenders destroyed 1,733 German aircraft in operations over Britain. The British victory came at a cost of 915 RAF aircraft lost and 415 pilots killed.

In the perspective of elapsed time, four factors stand out as having been key to the British victory: first, above all else, was Britain's indomitable will to win; second was radar, providing the RAF with the ability to detect the presence, size, and routes of the enemy; third was a well-organized, effectively run ground control system that enabled Fighter Command to direct its defensive forces where and when needed the most; and fourth was the Germans' own strategic shortcomings in scattering their efforts and failing to concentrate on the destruction of Fighter Command bases and vital aircraft manufacturing plants.

The summer of 1940 will forever stand as Britain's proudest season. Over the course of that unforgettable summer, a handful of blue-clad pilots faced off against Hitler's mighty, undefeated war machine and ensured that there would always be an England.

In Spitfires and Hurricanes, they flew where angels fear to fly. Routinely outnumbered, often overmatched, seldom outfought, they won an unwinnable battle against an unbeatable foe. To some, it was "a piece of cake"; to others, a trip to eternity. But to all, it was a superbly answered call to everlasting glory.

Glossary

A/A: Antiaircraft.

A/C: Aircraft.

Adlerangriff: Attack of the eagles.

Adler Tag: Eagle Day.

aerodrome, airdrome: Airfield or airport.

armistice: Temporary suspension of hostilities by agreement between opponents.

BBC: British Broadcasting Corporation.

BEF: British Expeditionary Force; British armed force abroad.

Bentley Priory: Fighter Command headquarters, the former residence of a religious order, near Stanmore.

blitzkrieg: Lightning war.

Bomber Command: Bomber division of the Royal Air Force.

Channel: The English Channel; narrow waterway separating England from the European continent.

Coastal Command: Coastal patrol division of the Royal Air Force.

contrail: Vapor trail left by an airplane or missile at high altitudes.

convoy: Group of ships or vehicles traveling under escort or together.

cowling: Removable engine cover.

deflection shooting: Controlled shooting by means of a gun sight that calculates the position of a target relative to the arrival time of a projectile.

depression: Period of low general economic activity, usually marked by increasing levels of unemployment.

dogfight: Battle between (usually two) aircraft.

Dunkirk: Port city in northern France; scene of mass evacuation of British and French troops before the fall of France.

Fascist: Member of extreme right-wing political party or government.

Fighter Command: Fighter division of the Royal Air Force.

flak: Exploding antiaircraft shells.

Führer: Leader; specifically, Adolf Hitler.

fuselage: The body of an airplane.

Gruppe: Group; a basic German flying unit, usually comprising three Staffeln.

HE bomb: Bomb containing an explosive such as TNT (a "high explosive") that generates gas rapidly upon detonation, with shattering effect.

House of Commons: Assembly of elected representatives in the British Parliament; equivalent to the U.S. House of Representatives.

Hun: German military opponent (after warlike Asiatic vandals who invaded Europe during the fourth and fifth centuries).

incendiary bomb: Bomb containing chemicals that ignite on bursting or on contact.

inflation: General increase in prices and fall in the purchasing power of money.

jettison: To throw overboard.

Kanakafu: *Kanalkampfführer;* leader of the German forces in the battle over the English Channel.

Karinhall: Goring's headquarters, described as a country showplace near Berlin.

Lebensraum: Literally, living space; more broadly, the right of Germany, as declared by Hitler, to acquire additional territory by expanding its borders.

Luftwaffe: Air force; specifically, the German air force.

Mein Kampf: *My Struggle*; the title of Hitler's autobiography.

Nazi: Abbreviated German version of National Socialist German Workers' Party, the political party of Adolf Hitler.

Operation Sea Lion: Code name for the German plan to invade England.

Peace Treaty of Versailles: The harsh settlement following World War I, imposed by the Allied powers upon Germany in 1919 at Versailles, France.

piece of cake: Something easily done; a cinch; a breeze.

port: Left-hand side.

radar: A system for detecting the presence (or position, movement, etc.) of objects by sending out short radio waves that the objects reflect.

RAF: Royal Air Force.

ready shack: Quarters where RAF pilots stood by on alert status.

Reichstag: Seat of German government; equivalent to U.S. Congress or British Parliament.

R/T: Radio telephone; radio/transmitter; receiver/transmitter.

scramble: Rush to take off and intercept enemy aircraft.

sector-station: Fighter Command airfield that serves as nerve center for command, control, communications, and intelligence.

sortie: A single flight by a single plane.

starboard: Right-hand side.

Staffel (plural, Staffeln): Element of usually nine German aircraft.

Strait of Dover: Narrowest section of the English Channel, between Dover and Calais.

strategy: The planning and directing of the entire operation of a war or campaign (*see also* tactics).

tactics: The art of placing or maneuvering forces skillfully in a battle (*see also* strategy).

Tannenberg: Code name for Nazi meeting at Kneibis in the Black Forest, where Operation Sea Lion was conceived.

Third Reich: Germany under the Nazi regime between 1933 and 1945.

Uxbridge: The headquarters of No. 11 Group, located on the western outskirts of London.

WAAF: Women's Auxiliary Air Force.

Wehrmacht: Army; specifically, the German army.

Weimar Republic: German regime established in accordance with the terms of the Treaty of Versailles; replaced by the Third Reich.

For Further Reading

John Batchelor and Bryan Cooper, *Fighter*. New York: Charles Scribner's Sons, 1973. An illustrated history of the fighter plane, from open-cockpit aircraft to modern jets.

Philip D. Caine, *American Pilots in the RAF: The World War II Eagle Squadrons*. New York: Brassey's (U.S.), 1993. A well-researched history of Americans flying for Britain, written by a retired U.S. Air Force general.

Christopher Chant, John F. Davis, Bill Gunston, Richard Humble, and Donald Macintyre, *The Encyclopedia of Air Warfare*. New York: Thomas Y. Crowell, 1975. Excellent illustrated history of war in the air.

Harold Faber, ed., *Luftwaffe: A History*. New York: Quadrangle/New York Times Book Company, 1977. An excellent history that reveals the inner workings of the Luftwaffe's high command.

Larry Forrester, *Fly for Your Life*. New York: Bantam Books, 1990. An exciting biography of RAF ace Stanford Tuck; reads like a novel.

Vern Haugland, *The Eagle Squadrons*. New York: Ziff-Davis Flying Books, 1979. A history of Yanks in the RAF during 1940–1942, written by a veteran war correspondent and aviation writer.

Robert Jackson, *Fighter Pilots of World War II*. New York: St. Martin's Press, 1976. Brief, exciting sketches of fourteen top fighter pilots in action during the Second World War.

Leonard Mosley, *"Battle of Britain": The Making of a Film*. New York: Ballantine Books, 1969. Documents the making of a famous movie about a famous battle, with interesting insights into the real fight.

Heinz J. Nowarra, *The Messerschmitt 109: A Famous German Fighter*. Los Angeles: Aero Publishers, 1963. The complete story of the design, development, and wartime role of Germany's most famous fighter plane.

Janusz Piekalkiewicz, *The Air War 1939–1945*. New York: Sterling Publishing, 1985. A history of aerial warfare, with a brief but interesting account of the Battle of Britain.

Alfred Price, *Fighter Aircraft*. New York: Sterling Publishing, 1989. A brief examination of the evolving tactics and techniques related to ever-improving fighter design and capability.

Alfred Price, *Luftwaffe Handbook 1939–1945*. New York: Charles Scribner's Sons, 1977. This short history focuses on the structure, tactics, and strategy of the German air force.

Bruce Robertson, *Spitfire—The Story of a Famous Fighter*. Fallbrook, CA: Aero Publishers, 1961. A fully illustrated and enormously detailed history of the only Allied fighter plane to remain in production throughout the whole of World War II.

Derek Robinson, *A Piece of Cake*. New York: Knopf, 1983. A piece of fiction but rich in accurate detail. The novel tells what it was truly like to fight in the Battle of Britain.

Edward H. Sims, *The Aces Talk*. New York: Ballantine Books, 1972. The story of fighter tactics and strategy and the pilots who helped to develop them.

Mike Spick, *The Ace Factor*. New York: Avon Books, 1988. Identifies and analyzes the elusive quality that separates aces from other pilots. A mini history of war in the air.

Colin Willock, *The Fighters*. Greenwich, CT: Fawcett Publications, 1973. Fiction founded on fact; World War II air action from both the British and German viewpoints.

Works Consulted

Ralph Barker and Time-Life Books editors, *The RAF at War*. Alexandria, VA: Time-Life Books, 1981. A beautifully illustrated and written account of the RAF during World War II.

Marcel Baudot, Henri Bernard, Hendrik Brugmans, Michael R.D. Foot, and Hans-Adolf Jacobsen, eds; Jesse Dilson, translator; Alvin D. Coox and Thomas R.H. Havens, additional material, *The Historical Encyclopedia of World War II*. New York: Facts on File, 1980. An overview of the Second World War with an excellent account of the Battle of Britain.

Paul Brickhill, *Reach for the Sky*. New York: Ballantine Books, 1967. The story of Sir Douglas Bader, Britain's great, legless fighter pilot; a remarkable biography of a remarkable man.

Winston Churchill, *Their Finest Hour*. Boston: Houghton Mifflin, 1949. Contains an account of the Battle of Britain that is a classic example of the distinguished author's unmatchable style.

R. Ernest Dupuy and Trevor N. Dupuy, *The Encyclopedia of Military History*. New York: Harper & Row, 1977. One of the great military reference books; contains a short but fine description of the Battle of Britain.

Trevor N. Dupuy, Curt John, and David L. Bongard, *The Harper Encyclopedia of Military Biography*. New York: Harper & Row, 1992. The researcher's sourcebook for information about the lives of major figures in military history.

Adolf Galland, *The First and the Last*. New York: Henry Holt, 1954. Germany's great fighter-general tells what it was like to fly for the Luftwaffe during World War II; authentic, dramatic nonfiction.

Edward Jablonski, *Airwar,* Vol. I. Garden City, NY: Doubleday, 1971. A well-researched, well-written pictorial history of the Second World War in the air; excellent coverage of the Battle of Britain and the blitz.

Robert Jackson, *Fighter! The Story of Air Combat 1936–1945*. New York: St. Martin's Press, 1979. Eleven true and exciting tales of action in the air, starting with the Spanish Civil War and extending through World War II.

Philip Kaplan and Richard Collier, *Their Finest Hour*. New York: Abbeville Press, 1989. A splendidly written and illustrated look back at the Battle of Britain, fifty years later; a marvelous work of aviation and military nostalgia.

John Killen, *A History of the Luftwaffe*. New York: Bantam Books, 1986. Interesting, thorough, yet fast-moving history of the Luftwaffe from 1914 through May 1945.

Roger Parkinson, *Summer, 1940: The Battle of Britain*. New York: David McKay, 1977. A beautifully rendered version of Britain's great air battle by a noted British historian.

William L. Shirer, *The Rise and Fall of the Third Reich*. New York: Simon & Schuster, 1960. The definitive book on Germany under Adolf Hitler with an informative section about Operation Sea Lion and the Battle of Britain.

Peter Townsend, *Duel of Eagles*. New York: Simon & Schuster, 1971. A former RAF squadron leader traces the development of the Royal Air Force and the Luftwaffe from World War I through the Battle of Britain.

Arthur Ward, *A Nation Alone*. London: Osprey Publishing, 1989. An illustrated and detailed study of England under siege; recaptures the flavor of that fateful summer in 1940.

Peter Young, ed., *The World Almanac of World War II*. New York: World Almanac, imprint of Pharos Books, 1986. This almanac offers a concise, calendar depiction of significant events during the Battle of Britain.

Appendix: Principal Aircraft in the Battle of Britain

Dornier Do 17z-2 "Flying Pencil"

The German trend toward fairly small, high-powered, highly loaded but versatile aircraft started with the Dornier Do 17. Twenty-five miles per hour faster than the RAF's biplane fighters at the time of its creation in 1937, the Do 17 was designed to eliminate the need for a fighter escort. It would, the Germans thought, evade enemy fighters by means of speed alone. This theory proved to be totally false, and the "Flying Pencil" (so named for its long, thin fuselage) fell in great numbers to the RAF's newer, single-winged Spitfire and Hurricane fighters.

Design of the Do 17 began in 1933 as part of Hitler's secret rearmament program. Under the guise of developing a fast postal plane that could carry six passengers, the Do 17's designers allowed for its easy conversion to what evolved into one of the Luftwaffe's best-known and most-used bombers. Either by design or oversight, the Do 17 later proved unacceptable for commercial use in that its narrow fuselage precluded passenger comfort.

The Do 17 established a design base for a whole series of variations and continually evolving alternative versions. It held a place of honor among the most vital of all Luftwaffe aircraft. The Do 17, in some form, remained in production throughout the war and saw action on practically all fronts.

Hawker Hurricane MK 1

The Hurricane shot down more enemy planes in the Battle of Britain than all other air and ground defenses combined. Upon first acquaintance, RAF ace Stanford Tuck called it "a flying brick, a great lumbering stallion." But he later admitted that "she was solid . . . steady as a rock . . . a wonderful gun platform." "It was strong," Pilot Officer Robert Doe agreed. "It could turn on a sixpence. It was a brutal machine where the guns were really fixed firmly."

The Hurricane established several respected "firsts" in its role as Britain's "workhorse" fighter: it was the first RAF monoplane fighter, the first fighter to mount eight machine guns, and the first fighter to break the 300-mile-per-hour barrier.

In terms of total victories during the Battle of Britain, the Hurricane also came in first, shooting down a whopping 80 percent of the RAF's recorded "kills" over Luftwaffe aircraft. Since Fighter Command used the Hurricanes mainly against German bombers, reserving the faster Spitfires for use against German fighters, the Hurricane's victory percentage is somewhat misleading. Still, an 80 percent piece of the action stands as a remarkable feat.

Constructed of wood, fabric, and metal framing, and powered by a Rolls-Royce Merlin engine, the sturdy Hurricane won the praises of flight mechanics as a "go anywhere, do anything plane."

Heinkel He 111P-2

As the first modern medium bomber introduced into the Luftwaffe, the He 111 bore the brunt of the bombing raids against Britain. It underwent continual design changes but maintained its place as a standard Luftwaffe bomber throughout the war.

Conceived by Walther and Siegfried Gunther, the leading Heinkel designers, the 111 was designed to meet specifications of Deutsche Lufthansa (Germany's civil air carrier) for a high-speed airliner. Included in Lufthansa's design guidelines were all the basic requirements for converting the aircraft into a Luftwaffe bomber. Like the Do 17 and various other German warplanes that formed a part of Germany's secret rearmament program, the He 111 evolved in the guise of a commercial aircraft.

Indeed, when the He 111 first appeared on public display at Tempelhof Airport, Berlin, on January 10, 1936, German newspapers acclaimed it as "the fastest machine in civil aviation." But its true role as a destructive force became clear all too soon.

On April 26, 1937, this "civil" aircraft gained worldwide notoriety. As part of the Condor Legion—a German volunteer air force that fought for Francisco Franco during the Spanish Civil War—several squadrons of He 111s bombed the defenseless little Basque town of Guernica out of existence. But why?

Questioned about Guernica during the war-crimes trials at Nuremberg in 1946, Luftwaffe chief Hermann Göring explained: Guernica had been a testing ground for the Luftwaffe. It was a pity; but we could not do otherwise, as we had nowhere else to try out our machines."

Göring showed no remorse. He was sentenced to death by the tribunal but committed suicide before the sentence could be carried out.

Junkers Ju 87B-2 "Stuka"

Germans variously called the Stuka (after *Sturzkampfflugzeug*, a term used to describe all dive-bombers) the scourge of Europe, the aircraft that conquered nations, and the supreme weapon. The RAF chaps called it "a piece of cake." Deadly when unopposed, as it was in Europe, the Stuka became dead meat for Hurricanes and Spitfires over Britain. Göring ordered the Stuka withdrawn from operations over Britain on August 19, 1940.

Spearheading Hitler's "lightning war" in Europe, the Ju 87 Stuka helped establish the myth of Luftwaffe invincibility during the first months of the Second World War. Its fearsome inverted-gull-winged appearance and its soul-searing shriek when diving on target wreaked horror and havoc on thousands of hapless victims. Few World War II aircraft achieved so much acclaim for failure as did the absurdly ugly Stuka.

In fairness to the airplane that introduced the blitzkrieg concept, however, it should be stated that the Stuka eventually proved to be a deadly "tank killer" on the Eastern Front. Hans-Ulrich Rudel, the Luftwaffe's most famous Stuka pilot, flew 2,530 combat missions in the ugly dive-bomber. Known as the

"Eagle of the Eastern Front," Rudel personally destroyed 3 Soviet ships, 70 landing craft, and 519 tanks.

Junkers Ju 88A-1

Probably the most versatile Luftwaffe aircraft, the Ju 88 originated in 1936 and stayed in production throughout the war. More than sixteen thousand rolled off German assembly lines. In addition to its bombing role, the remarkable Ju 88 operated successfully as a heavy fighter, night fighter, close-support, and reconnaissance aircraft.

Design of the Ju 88 was started after Inspector-General of the Luftwaffe Erhard Milch asked representatives of the German aircraft industry to submit proposals to the German Air Ministry for a *schnellbomber*—a medium bomber with the speed of a fighter.

The very fast, slim, twin-engined airplane that resulted from Milch's request was soon fitted with dive brakes to oblige former World War I flying ace Ernst Udet's wishes for a twin-engined dive-bomber. Udet, by then a colonel in the Luftwaffe's Technical Department, had become Germany's leading supporter of the dive-bomber and the driving force behind its development.

Milch took credit for the Ju 88, however, calling it his "wonder bomber." The title was well deserved, as the versatile aircraft was destined to become the backbone of the Luftwaffe. Like the Dornier Do 17, the Ju 88 underwent many design changes and improvements and, in one version or another, operated on all fronts throughout the entire war.

Messerschmitt Me 109E-4

Many aviation historians argue that the Me 109 was the greatest fighter aircraft of all time. More than thirty-five thousand were manufactured between 1936 and 1945. The 109 is often referred to with a "Bf" prefix (derived from the name of Willy Messerschmitt's aircraft company *Bayerische Flugzeugwerke AG*) rather than the more popularly used "Me" designator. Comparing the 109 to the British Hurricane, German ace Adolf Galland said, "We outstripped them in speed, rate of climb, armament."

Describing the Me 109, RAF squadron leader Peter Townsend wrote: "It was a faster fighter, armed with two 20-mm cannon and two 7.9-mm machine guns—compared to the eight machine guns of the RAF's Hurricanes and Spitfires. It was less maneuverable than our fighters, but its Daimler Benz engine was equipped with fuel injection, enabling it to go abruptly into a dive from level flight. With us, the Merlin [engine] cut out momentarily under 'negative G,' [reverse gravitational force] as in going over the top of a switch-back [loop], and lost us a few precious seconds."

Conceived in the summer of 1934, the Me 109 served as a model for the other pure fighters that came out of World War II. Throughout the war it competed in a technological race with the British Spitfire, with both aircraft undergoing continual design improvements in the struggle to gain control of the air.

Messerschmitt Me 110C-4

Originally designed as a long-range fighter escort for bombers, the Me 110 was underpowered and underarmed. After Hurricanes and Spitfires had been cutting the 110s to pieces over Britain for months, Göring decided to try using them as fighter-bombers. Basically not a good airframe, the 110 also failed in this dual bombing role. Despite many shortcomings, the aircraft remained in production until 1945.

Luftwaffe chief Hermann Göring at first took great pride in this twin-engined fighter and expected great things from it. So convinced was Göring of the 110's destructive powers that he nicknamed the fighter *Zerstörer* (Destroyer). But when matched against Britain's faster, more maneuverable single-engined fighters in the Battle of Britain, the "Destroyers" managed to escape their own destruction only by forming a defensive circle. Each 110 would then protect the tail of the air-

craft in front of him, until the 110 pilots could shift their circle out of harm's way.

A later G4 model of the Me 110 achieved some success as a night fighter. This success increased significantly with the introduction of a new Liechtenstein-type aircraft radar. The new devices helped the 110 night fighters to score effectively against Allied bombers when the Allies commenced massive bombing raids on Germany. The 110's role as a night fighter ended in early 1944 with the appearance of more efficient fighters.

Supermarine Spitfire MK 1A

The Mark 1A model was the main version of Spitfire that defended England against the Luftwaffe during the Battle of Britain. British ace Pilot Officer Stanford Tuck described the Spitfire as "thirty feet of wicked beauty . . . with practically no relation to any of the aircraft I'd flown previously."

Britain's great legless ace Pilot Officer Douglas Bader said that the Spitfire handled "like a highly-strung thoroughbred."

The Spitfire, nimbler and faster than the Hawker Hurricane, its more rugged comrade-in-arms, reached its maximum speed of 362 miles per hour at a height of nineteen thousand feet. Heavily armed with four .303-inch Browning machine guns mounted in each wing, the Spitfire became the fighter plane most feared by Luftwaffe pilots.

Of the Spitfire's performance during the Battle of Britain, Luftwaffe field marshal General Albert Kesselring said, "Only the Spitfires bothered us."

Conceived by British aircraft designer Reginald Mitchell, the Spitfire's classic lines seemed to blend with nature's vision of perfect flight characteristics. A total of 20,334 Spitfires in various versions were produced during World War II. The Spitfire remains to this day the dominant symbol of the RAF's courageous defense of Britain in the summer of 1940.

Index

Adler Tag (Eagle Day)
  Adlerangriff (attack of the
    eagles, 31-32
  preparation for, 31-32
  Sailor's August Eleventh, 33-35
  three days of the eagle, 41-53
    all Air Fleets in one day,
      45-51
Aitken, William Maxwell. *See*
  Beaverbrook, Lord
Anti-Aircraft Command, 69

Bader, Douglas, 70-71, 91
Balloon Command, 69
Barclay, George, 65-66
Battle of Britain
  Battle of Britain Day
    (September 15), 65-75
    aftermath of, 75
  Beaverbrook, importance of,
    18, 29-30, 60, 73
  Big Wing strategy controversy,
    60-61
  cessation of daylight raids, 48,
    78
  chronology of events, 8
  fighter strength at start, 28
  first bombing of London, 53
  first day: July 10, 1940, 21-24
  pilot/plane tolls
    daily tallies, 33, 40, 48, 51,
      53, 59, 62, 66, 67, 75, 77
    final score, 84
  summing up, 84
  terror bombings on civilians, 62
    British retaliation in kind,
      63-64
  winding down, 77-84
  see also Adler Tag; Dowding, Sir
    Hugh C.T.; London; maps; Park,
    Keith; radar
Beaverbrook, Lord, invaluable
  contributions of, 18, 29-30, 60
  Ministry of Aircraft Production,
    73
Berlin, retaliatory bombing of,
  63-64
Big Wing strategy, 70, 71-73

controversy over, 60-61, 81-84
Dowding and Park's resistance
  to, 60-61, 73
  price they paid, 81-84
Blenheim fighters, 48
Boorman, Pratt, 62
Boulton-Paul Defiant (fighter), 13
Brand, Christopher, 50, 60
British Intelligence information,
  69
Buckingham Palace bombed, 70
Bulmer, G.G.R., 23

Carne, Daphne, 39
chronology of events, 8
Churchill, Clementine, 68
Churchill, Winston
  on Battle of Britain Day, 75
  on courage of Londoners, 78
  Dowding and, 26-27
  finest hour speech, 15, 17
  further praise of Fighter
    Command, 77
  The Gathering Storm, 9
  never . . . in human conflict
    speech, 54
  vows never to surrender, 14-15
circle maneuver, 35, 91
Civilian Repair Organization, 60,
  73
Crisp, J.L., 43
Crook, David M., 16-17, 44, 51,
  62

defensive circle maneuver, 35, 91
Defiant (fighter), 13, 48
Do 17. *See Dornier Do 17*
Donahue, Art, 60
Dornier Do 17
  as "Flying Pencil," 35
  history and description, 89
Douglas, Sholto, 61, 82
Dowding, Sir Hugh C.T., 18, 48,
  50, 55, 66-67, 76
  control of other units, 69
  resistance to Big Wing, 73

price he paid, 82
reward for services rendered,
  81-84
status and strategy, 26-30
strategic dilemma, 59-62
Dunkirk
  evacuation at, 14-15
  RAF activities and losses, 27

Eagle Day. *See Adler Tag*

Faviell, Frances, 39
Fink, Johannes, 22, 29, 41
Fiske, Billy, 56
"Flying Pencil." *See Dornier Do 17*
Foch, Ferdinand, 9
Franco, Francisco, 90
Franz Ferdinand, archduke of
  Austria-Hungary, 10
Fuch (German pilot), 23

Galland, Adolf, 46, 91
  on admiration of British pilots,
    71
  on Battle of Britain, 83
  on Ju 87s, 29
  on modification of Me 110s, 34,
    78
  on need for Spitfires, 78
  on strain of pilot casualties,
    58-59
Gardner, Charles, 24
The Gathering Storm (Churchill),
  9
Geischecker (German radio
  operator), 48
George VI, king of England, 70
Göring, Hermann, 18, 22, 35
  attack of the eagles, 31-32
  early strategy, 29-30
  on Guernica destruction, 90
  plans to destroy RAF, 20-21
  sentence/suicide, 90
  strategic errors
    allocation of fighters, 53
    Me 110 modification, 91

stopped low-level attacks, 59
underestimation of radar, 36, 40, 54
terror bombings on civilians, 62
Gotha bombers (World War I), 69
Grigg, Sir Edward, 24-25
Gunther, Siegfried, 89
Gunther, Walther, 89
Gustavus V, king of Sweden, 18

Handrick, Gotthardt, 44
Hawker Hurricane. *See* Hurricane (fighter)
Heinkel He 111, 45-47
history and description, 89-90
Helbig, Jochen, 50-51
Hintze, Otto, 35, 37
Hitler, Adolf
chancellorship, dictatorship, 11
"Directive No. 16" (preparation for invasion of England), 24, 26
"Directive No. 17" (conduct of attack on England), 26
indecision/delay on invasion of England, 17-20, 68
postpones invasion indefinitely, 75
Lebensraum and, 11-12
plans Operation Sea Lion, 15, 18-20
strategic error, divert bombing to London, 67
see also World War II
Holmes, Ray, 70
Hurricane (fighter)
compared to Ju 87s, 29, 53
description, 89
record number of kills, 89
Huth (German pilot), 23

Ismay, Hastings, 51-52, 54

Jodl, Alfred, 18-20
Jones, John Paul, 48
Jones, Len, 79, 81
Ju 87 (Stuka)

described, 90
vulnerability to British fighters, 29, 53
Ju 88
history and description, 90
multiple uses of, 90

Kanakafu, 22
Kesselring, Albert, 20-21, 45, 67, 91

Lane, Bryan, 71
Lebensraum, 11-12
Leigh-Mallory, Trafford 48-49, 75
Big Wing strategy, 60-61, 73
Dowding and, 28-29
lack of cooperation, 60-61
revenge, 82-83
Linke (German pilot), 47
London
the blitz, 78-81
Buckingham Palace hit, 70
civilian casualties, 66, 67, 81
fifty-seven nights of bombs, 64, 78-81
first bombing of, 53
first intentional bombing, 65
300 tons of bombs, 66
terror bombings begin, 63
total civilian casualties, 81
Luftwaffe
kills/losses in Battle of Britain, 84
superiority of numbers at war's start, 13
Luton (England) *News*, 80
Lutz, Martin, 35, 37

Maginot Line, 13
Malan, Adolphus "Sailor," 42, 51
Sailor's August Eleventh, 33-35
maps
bombing of British airfields, 52
British and German airfields, 67
British Fighter Command group areas, 57
British radar installations, 37

Operationi Sea Lion, 21
Martini, Wolfgang, 35, 40
Mass Observation (pollsters' report), 80
Mayers (British pilot), 42-43
Me 109
history and description, 90-91
comparison with British fighters, 91
Me 110
comparison with British fighters, 25, 53
defensive circle maneuver, 35, 91
first dogfight over England, 16-17
history and description 91
modified to fighter-bomber, 34, 53, 91
problems due to short range, 71
use as night fighter, 91
Mein Kampf (Hitler), 11
Messerschmitt, Willy, 91
Messerschmitts (fighters). *See* Me 109; Me 110
Mickelthwait Height Correction Attachment, 69
Milch, Erhard, 31, 90
military twenty-four-hour clock, 10
Ministry of Aircraft Production, 73
Mitchell, Reginald, 91
Murrow, Edward R., 58, 81
Mussolini, Benito, 24

Nicholson, James, Victoria Cross recipient, 57
Norton Newell, Sir Cyril Louis, 33
Novi (Polish pilot), 44
Nuremberg war crimes trials, 90

Observer Corps, 69
Mickelthwait Height Correction Attachment, 69
Operation Sea Lion, 15
Hitler's indecisions about, 17-20, 68

map, 21
postponed indefinitely, 75
preparations for, 26
Outzmann (German pilot), 35

Park, Keith, 18, 49, 51, 59-60,
   67-69, 73
   resistance to Big Wing, 61
      price he paid, 82
   reward for services rendered,
      81-83
   status at start of Battle of
      Britain, 28-29
Park, Mungo, 21, 35
Peel, J.R.A., 32
phony war, benefit for RAF, 12-13
*A Practical Guide for the
   Householder and Air-Raid
   Warden*, 80

radar
   as early primary targets, 35-37
   description, 36
   Görings underestimation of,
      36, 40, 54
   importance, 30, 36, 40, 69
   Liechtenstein-type aircraft radar,
      91
   map of installations, 37
Richter (German pilot), 47-48
Roessiger, Wilhelm, 35, 37
Royal Air Force
   activities/losses at Dunkirk, 27
   benefit from phony war, 12-13
   early use of Defiant fighters, 13
   fighters at start of Battle of
      Britain, 28
   Görings plan to destroy, 20-21
   kills/losses in Battle of Britain,
      84

Rubensdörf, Walter, 34-35, 37,
   39, 52-53
Rudel, Hans-Ulrich, 90
Rundstedt, Gerd von, 19

Sailor's August Eleventh, 33-35
Sample, John, 73-74
Saul, Richard Ernest, 46
Schicklgruber, Adolf. *See* Hitler,
   Adolf
Schlund (German gunner), 51
Schmid, Josef "Beppo," 72
seaplanes, stage failed mock
   attack, 46
sector, defined, 55
sector stations, defined, 56
Shirer, William L., 12, 63
sortie, defined, 30
Sperrle, Hugo, 20, 31, 45, 50
Spitfire (fighter)
   described, 91
   versus Ju 87s, 29
Staaken bombers (World War I),
   69
Stephen, Mackay, 35
Stevenson (RAF pilot) 51
Stirling (bomber), 50
Stuka. *See* Ju 87
Stumpf, Hans-Jürgen, 20, 31, 46,
   48
Supermarine Spitfire. *See* Spitfire
   (fighter)

terror bombings on civilians, 62
   British retaliation in kind, 63-64
   see also London
Third Reich, 10-11
Townsend, Peter, 18, 25, 73
   his song of survival, 55-56
   on injustice to heroes, 82

on Me 109, 91
Trautloft, Hannes, 23
Tuck, Stanford, 70, 89
twenty-four-hour clock, 10

Udet, Ernst, 90

von Chamier-Glisczinski
   (German pilot), 50

WAAF (Women's Auxiliary Air
   Force), 38-39, 47
war crimes trials at Nuremberg,
   90
Watson-Watt, Robert, 36
Weimar Republic, 10-11
Westmacott, Innes, 60
Whitley (bomber), 48
Women's Auxiliary Air Force
   (WAAF), 38-39, 47
World War I, Treaty of
   Versailles, 9-10
World War II
   early course
      annexations without battle,
         11-12
      blitzkrieg of Poland, 12
      phony war, period of, 12-13
      Scandinavia, Lowlands
         invaded, 13
      Maginot Line skirted, 13-14
      evacuation at Dunkirk, 14-15
      Paris falls, 15
   preceding events
      Lebensraum, 11-12
      Third Reich, 10-11
      Treaty of Versailles, 9-10
   see also Hitler, Adolf

Picture Credits

Cover photo by UPI/Bettmann Newsphotos

Archive Photos, 19, 25, 28 (center), 40, 49 (right)

Hulton Deutsch Collection Limited, 30 (left), 50, 56 (right), 77

Imperial War Museum, 26, 34 (left), 45, 47 (right), 54, 56 (left), 61, 72, 83

Library of Congress, 17, 29, 34 (right), 38, 53, 58 (right), 65 (right), 74 (right), 80, 81

National Archives, 11, 12, 13 (both), 15, 20 (bottom), 21, 23 (both), 24, 30 (right), 32, 33, 36, 43, 47 (left), 49 (left), 58 (left), 59, 63, 64, 65 (left), 68 (both), 70, 71, 74 (left), 79, 84

Courtesy of the Simon Wiesenthal Center Beit HaShoah Museum of Tolerance Library/Archives, Los Angeles, CA, 20 (top)

UPI/Bettmann Newsphotos, 22, 28 (left, right), 42, 66

About the Author

Earle Rice Jr. attended San Jose City College and Foothill College on the San Francisco peninsula after having served nine years with the U.S. Marine Corps.

He has authored nine other books for young adults, including adaptations of *Dracula* and *All Quiet on the Western Front*. Mr. Rice most recently wrote *The Cuban Revolution* for Lucent Books. He has also written articles and short stories and worked for several years as a technical writer.

Mr. Rice recently retired from the aerospace industry, where he worked as a senior design engineer. He lives in Julian, California, with his wife, daughter, granddaughter, two cats, and a dog.